The U.S. Supreme Court: A Very Short Introduction

VERY SHORT INTRODUCTIONS are for anyone wanting a stimulating and accessible way into a new subject. They are written by experts, and have been translated into more than 45 different languages.

The series began in 1995, and now covers a wide variety of topics in every discipline. The VSI library currently contains over 600 volumes—a Very Short Introduction to everything from Psychology and Philosophy of Science to American History and Relativity—and continues to grow in every subject area.

Very Short Introductions available now:

Available soon:

For more information visit our web site

www.oup.com/vsi/

Linda Greenhouse

THE U.S.
SUPREME
COURT

A Very Short Introduction

SECOND EDITION

OXFORD
UNIVERSITY PRESS

Oxford University Press is a department of the University of Oxford.
It furthers the University's objective of excellence in research, scholarship,
and education by publishing worldwide. Oxford is a registered trade mark of
Oxford University Press in the UK and certain other countries.

Published in the United States of America by Oxford University Press
198 Madison Avenue, New York, NY 10016, United States of America.

Library of Congress Control Number: 2019955818

ISBN 978-0-19-007981-9

3 5 7 9 8 6 4

Printed and bound by CPI Group (UK) Ltd, Croydon, CR0 4YY

For Gene and Hannah

Contents

List of illustrations

All illustrations are from the collection of the Supreme Court of the United States with the exception of the photograph of William O. Douglas, which is from the Library of Congress.

Acknowledgments

Steve Petteway, the Supreme Court's photographer, was generous with his time in helping me select most of the photographs that appear in this book. This is one of three of my books to have received the benefit of Steve's professional enthusiasm before his retirement in 2017, and I thank him once again. I thank Sanford Levinson for his comments on the original manuscript, and my husband and fellow law teacher, Eugene Fidell, for having read each chapter as it emerged. My editor, Nancy Toff, recruited me for this project and helped me to envision a world full of curious readers who want to know more about the U.S. Supreme Court. I'm glad she did.

Chapter 1
Origins

"The judicial power of the United States, shall be vested in one Supreme Court, and in such inferior courts as the Congress may from time to time ordain and establish."

With those words—the opening sentence of the Constitution's Article III—the document's Framers announced the birth of an institution then unknown to the world, a national court with the authority to decide cases "arising under" the country's Constitution and laws. Precisely what that authority would mean in practice—what the Supreme Court's role would be with respect to the two elected branches of the new government—was far from clear when the Constitution was drafted in 1787. That role remains disputed even today, when Supreme Court nominees are routinely asked by members of the Senate Judiciary Committee to disavow all interest in using the Court's authority in a manner that might be described as "judicial activism."

This book is not intended primarily as a work of history. Its aim is to enable readers to understand how the Supreme Court of the United States operates today. But while detailed knowledge of the Court's history is not required for that purpose, acquaintance with the Court's origins helps appreciate the extent to which the Supreme Court that we know today has been the author of its own history. From the beginning, it has filled in the blanks of Article

III by defining its own power. In the process, the Court has defied Alexander Hamilton's prediction in Federalist No. 78 (one of the eighty-five essays in the Federalist Papers, written to rally public support for the Constitution's ratification) that lacking "influence over either the sword or the purse," and possessing "neither force nor will, but merely judgment," the judiciary would prove to be the "least dangerous branch." That process of self-definition continues today.

The Articles of Confederation that the new United States ratified in 1781 provided neither a national judicial system nor an executive branch. (There was a single national court, the Court of Appeals in Cases of Capture, with jurisdiction limited to disputes over captured ships. The Congress also had the power to establish special courts to resolve boundary disputes between states; such a court had only sat once.) Every state had its own system of courts, as the states do today. Citizens of the new nation had feared that a federal court system with general jurisdiction would threaten the sovereignty of the loosely confederated states. But to the delegates who assembled in Philadelphia in 1787 to revise the national charter, the absence of a national judicial system was one of the decentralized government's more obvious failings.

The Constitutional Convention quickly agreed to the proposal of Governor Edmund Randolph of Virginia for a national government of three branches: legislative, executive, and judicial. Randolph's resolution "that a national Judiciary be established" passed unanimously. Debating and defining the powers of Congress in Article I and of the president in Article II consumed much of the delegates' attention and energy. Central provisions of Article III were the product of compromise and, in its fewer than five hundred words, the article left important questions unresolved. Lacking agreement on a role for lower courts, for example, the delegates simply left it to Congress to decide how to structure them. The number of justices remained unspecified. Article III itself makes no reference to the office of chief justice, to whom the Constitution (in Article I) assigns only one specific duty, that of presiding over a Senate trial in a presidential impeachment. The convention debated at length over how the members of the Supreme Court should be selected, eventually settling on nomination by the president and confirmation by the Senate. By providing that federal judges "shall hold their offices during good Behaviour," the delegates intended to protect judicial independence.

But independence to do what, exactly? The delegates were aware that the supreme courts of several states were exercising the power of judicial review, invalidating legislative acts that, in the judges' view, violated provisions of the state's constitution. The Massachusetts Supreme Judicial Court, interpreting the Massachusetts Constitution of 1780, had invoked this power to declare slavery unconstitutional within the commonwealth. Courts in Virginia, North Carolina, New Jersey, New York, and Rhode Island had also exercised judicial review, sometimes generating public controversy, during the pre-Constitution period.

Although the delegates appear to have assumed that the federal courts would exercise some form of judicial review over federal and state laws, Article III says nothing explicit on the subject. It states in broad terms that the federal courts' judicial power "shall extend to all cases, in law and equity, arising under this Constitution, the laws of the United States, and treaties." It then goes on to list specific types of disputes over which the federal courts may exercise jurisdiction: cases between states; cases between a state and citizens of another state, or between citizens of different states; "controversies to which the United States shall be a party"; admiralty and maritime disputes; cases involving ambassadors and other foreign diplomats; and cases between a state or its citizens and the government or residents of a foreign state.

For the Supreme Court specifically, Article III makes a distinction between "original" and "appellate" jurisdiction—between the Supreme Court as a court of first resort for cases involving states or foreign diplomats, and the Court as the recipient of appeals from lower courts in all other cases. Given the initial absence of lower courts, this distinction must have seemed quite arcane to readers of the judiciary article. It would shortly prove highly significant.

Once the Constitution was ratified, Congress quickly turned to the task of setting up a court system within the Article III framework. The Judiciary Act of 1789, often called the First Judiciary Act, established two tiers of lower courts: thirteen district courts that followed state lines, each with its own district judge, and three circuit courts, for the Eastern, Middle, and Southern Circuits. But the Judiciary Act did not provide for judges to staff the circuit courts. Instead, the circuits would be staffed during their two annual sittings by two Supreme Court justices and one district judge. This system required the justices to "ride circuit," an onerous duty under primitive conditions of interstate transportation, and one that early justices keenly resented. Hannah Cushing, the wife of Justice William Cushing, referred to herself and her husband as "traveling machines." Despite the justices' frequent complaints, however, this system lasted, in somewhat modified form, for more than a century, until Congress established fully staffed circuit courts (known today as United States Courts of Appeals, of which there are currently thirteen) in the Evarts Act of 1891.

The first Supreme Court, consisting of five associate justices and Chief Justice John Jay, a prominent New York lawyer from a distinguished family and a co-author of the Federalist Papers, began its work of self-definition almost immediately. Three of the associate justices, John Rutledge of South Carolina, James Wilson of Pennsylvania, and John Blair Jr. of Virginia, had been delegates to the Constitutional Convention. All were acutely aware of the

Court's place in the Constitution's design of separated powers. (President George Washington later appointed two more Constitutional Convention veterans to the Court, William Paterson of New Jersey and Oliver Ellsworth of Connecticut.) One early turning point came in 1793, when Secretary of State Thomas Jefferson sent the Supreme Court a letter on behalf of President Washington requesting help in resolving questions of interpretation that had arisen under the 1778 treaty between France and the United States. The letter posed twenty-nine specific questions. Judges of the state courts then commonly offered—as several still do—"advisory opinions" of the sort the president sought. But Chief Justice Jay and the associate justices viewed the request as falling outside the jurisdiction of the federal courts. In a letter to the president, the Court responded: "The lines of separation drawn by the Constitution between the three departments of the government—their being in certain respects checks upon each other—and our being judges of a court in the last resort—are considerations which afford strong arguments against the propriety of our extrajudicially deciding the questions alluded to."

This early rejection of an advisory role established a lasting principle: that the federal courts have the constitutional power to decide only those questions that arise in the context of disputes between opposing parties. The principle is easier to state than to apply, and the Court has spent the subsequent two centuries elaborating on it. Even today, the contours of what is often referred to as the "Article III jurisdiction" of the federal courts remain contested. The important points here are simply these: that questions concerning the federal courts' jurisdiction are anchored deeply in the nation's constitutional origins, and that the Supreme Court itself has provided the answers.

The Supreme Court met for the first time on February 2, 1790, in New York City, the country's first capital. The Court's meeting place was the Merchants Exchange (sometimes referred to as the

1. **The Old Merchants Exchange Building. Sometimes called the Royal Exchange, this was the Supreme Court's first home. The Court met in this building in lower Manhattan for the first time on February 2, 1790.**

Royal Exchange) building in lower Manhattan, the first of several locations that served as a home for the Supreme Court until the justices got their own building on Capitol Hill in 1935.

After a year in New York, the Court moved to Philadelphia, sitting first in the State House and then in the city's newly constructed city hall, where the justices shared space with the mayor's court. After nine years in Philadelphia, the Court moved along with the rest of the national government to the new capital in Washington, DC, in 1800. There, the Court operated for the next 135 years from the Capitol building. That the president and Congress were able to move into their own homes by 1800, while the Supreme Court lacked its own real estate until nearly the middle of the twentieth century, certainly suggests that the Court, and the branch that it was to head, began life in something less than equal partnership with the other two branches. It would be up to the Court itself to establish parity, something it achieved by giving itself dominion over the Constitution.

In the beginning, the prospect seemed distant that the Court would matter much at all. During its first two terms, February and August 1790, it had almost nothing to do. A year after its first session, the Court finally received its first case, but the case settled before argument. Six months later, in August 1791, the Court received a second case, an appeal in a commercial dispute. The justices heard arguments, but then declared that a procedural irregularity in the appeal barred them from proceeding to a decision. Not until 1792 did the Supreme Court begin issuing opinions.

In the early years, the justices worked hardest in their capacity as judges of the circuit courts, which had growing dockets due to their original jurisdiction over major federal crimes. It was in the circuit courts that the justices fleshed out some important principles of federal law and jurisdiction. One such instance came in 1792 in *Hayburn's Case*. A new law, the Invalid Pensions Act, directed the circuit courts to act as pension boards and determine the pension claims of injured Revolutionary War veterans. The justices, as circuit judges, refused to exercise this new grant of jurisdiction. The problem was that any determination by the court that a veteran was entitled to a pension would be subject to review by the secretary of war. In the justices' view, this added layer of executive branch review would turn the judicial determination into a nonjudicial act. Justices sitting on each of the three circuits wrote separately to President Washington explaining why they could not carry out the assigned duty. "Such revision and controul [*sic*] we deemed radically inconsistent with the independence of that judicial power which is vested in the courts," Justices James Wilson and John Blair, sitting on the Middle Circuit, explained in their letter. The attorney general appealed to the Supreme Court, which heard arguments but never issued a decision, because

Congress revised the offending statute in the meantime. Was *Hayburn's Case*, then, the first instance of the Supreme Court declaring an act of Congress unconstitutional? Not formally. But the dispute received wide attention and could have left little doubt in the public's mind that these justices would be zealous guardians of the jurisdictional boundaries that they understood the Constitution to have drawn.

The next year, the Court decided what is generally viewed as the major case of the early years. The decision, *Chisholm v. Georgia* (1793), provoked an immediate backlash, in the form of the first constitutional amendment to be ratified after the ten amendments of the Bill of Rights. The case was a suit by a merchant in South Carolina against the state of Georgia for a Revolutionary War debt. The plaintiff sued directly in the Supreme Court under the provision of Article III that gave the Court jurisdiction over suits between a state and a citizen of a different state. The Court rejected Georgia's argument that as a sovereign state it was immune from suit without its consent. When Georgia refused to appear, the Court entered a default judgment against it.

The five justices in the majority (there was one dissent) each wrote a separate opinion, as was the custom. The opinions constituted a decision that was highly nationalist in tone. "As to the purposes of the union, therefore, Georgia is not a sovereign state," wrote Justice Wilson. Not surprisingly, the states were alarmed by this development, and a constitutional amendment to overrule the decision was introduced two days later. In 1798, the Eleventh Amendment received final ratification, providing that the jurisdiction of the federal courts "shall not be construed to extend" to cases brought by citizens of one state against another state. Despite that seemingly conclusive language, the scope of state immunity from suit was far from settled, and remains a contested question even today.

Chief Justice Jay, who had run unsuccessfully for governor of New York while serving on the Court, was elected governor in 1795 and resigned his office. A New York newspaper approvingly described the chief justice's election as governor as a "promotion." Washington nominated John Rutledge of South Carolina, who had previously been confirmed to a position as an associate justice but had resigned without ever taking his seat, in order to become chief justice of the South Carolina Court of Common Pleas. This time, Rutledge agreed to serve and accepted a recess appointment, but the Senate refused to confirm him. Because Rutledge did serve in the position of chief justice from August 12 until December 15, 1795, he is counted as the country's second chief justice.

Washington next nominated a sitting associate justice, William Cushing, whom the Senate promptly confirmed. But he declined to take his seat on the ground of poor health. The president's next nomination, of Oliver Ellsworth of Connecticut, was successful. He took his seat as the third chief justice in March 1796, and served until resigning in ill health on December 15, 1800. President John Adams then offered John Jay his old job back. But Jay, who by then had served two terms as New York's governor, declined, observing that he was "perfectly convinced" that the federal judicial system was fundamentally "defective" and could never "acquire the public confidence and respect which, as the last resort of the justice of the nation, it should possess."

This was the inauspicious background for the nomination by John Adams of John Marshall, his secretary of state, to be the nation's fourth chief justice. Marshall, a Virginian and combat veteran of the Revolutionary War, was forty-five years old, until this day the youngest person ever to assume the office (the next youngest was John G. Roberts Jr., who became chief justice in 2005 at the age of fifty). He was a national figure, having helped lead the effort in Virginia to ratify the Constitution and later having undertaken an important diplomatic mission to France. He was the oldest of fifteen children, a fact that may help explain his natural leadership qualities. Not infrequently, Marshall is mistakenly referred to as the first chief justice. The mistake is understandable. Taking his seat in February 1801, he served for more than thirty-four years until his death on July 6, 1835. He left the Court a transformed institution, no longer the stepsister of the other two branches. To the dismay of Thomas Jefferson, to whom Marshall administered the presidential oath of office on March 4, 1801, the Marshall Court embraced a strongly nationalist vision of the country and a

2. Chief Justice John Marshall. This portrait of the fourth Chief Justice was painted by Rembrandt Peale and has hung in several locations at the Court.

willingness to harness the Constitution, and the Court's own authority as its primary interpreter, in the service of that vision.

Marbury v. Madison, the Marshall Court's best-known case, and one of the most famous in Supreme Court history, was decided early in the chief justice's tenure, on February 24, 1803. It grew out of the tense and messy transition of power from the Adams Federalists to the Jeffersonian Republicans after the election of 1800. The Federalist-populated courts were a particular target of the victorious Republicans, especially after the outgoing Federalist Congress created forty-two new judicial positions for President Adams to fill during his waning weeks in office.

A Maryland tax collector, William Marbury, had received one of these "midnight" appointments as a justice of the peace for the District of Columbia. The Senate confirmed Marbury's appointment along with the dozens of others. But in order to take office, the newly confirmed judicial officers needed to receive the actual commission, a piece of paper that Marbury had not received by the time the Adams administration left office. President Jefferson's secretary of state, James Madison, refused to deliver the commission. Marbury, who had been active in Federalist political circles, filed suit directly in the Supreme Court. He sought a writ of mandamus, a judicial order commanding the delivery of his commission. It seemed a readily available remedy, because Congress in the Judiciary Act of 1789 had explicitly provided that citizens could go directly to the Supreme Court to seek a writ of mandamus against a federal official.

As a legal matter, then, the case seemed straightforward enough. But it was also highly political, and it placed the authority of the Supreme Court on the line. Madison was seen as likely to defy a direct order to give Marbury his commission. How could the Supreme Court uphold the rule of law without provoking a confrontation with the executive branch that could leave the Court permanently weakened?

Origins

11

Marshall's solution was to assert the Court's power without directly exercising it. His opinion for a unanimous Court—speaking in one voice in the new Marshall style, rather than through a series of separate concurring opinions as in the past—held that Marbury was due his commission but that the Court could not order it delivered. That was because the grant of "original" jurisdiction to the Supreme Court in Article III did not include writs of mandamus. Section 13 of the Judiciary Act, in which Congress gave the Court jurisdiction to decide original mandamus actions like Marbury's, was therefore unconstitutional and no mandamus could be issued. The decision gave the Court a measure of insulation at a time of political turmoil; without an order, the Jefferson administration had nothing to complain about. The decision's significance, of course, lay in the Court's assertion of authority to review the constitutionality of acts of Congress. "It is emphatically the province and duty of the judicial department to say what the law is," Marshall declared—a line that the Court has invoked throughout its history, down to the present. In the guise of modestly disclaiming authority to act, the Court had assumed for itself great power.

The full extent of that power was not immediately apparent. In fact, only six days later, with Chief Justice Marshall not participating, the Court avoided a possible constitutional confrontation. Voting 5–0 in *Stuart v. Laird* (1803), the justices upheld Congress's repeal of the Judiciary Act of 1801, a move some historians see as reflecting the Court's unwillingness to test the full dimensions of the power it had just claimed for itself. More than half a century would pass before the Supreme Court again declared an act of Congress unconstitutional. That was the *Dred Scott* decision of 1857 (*Scott v. Sandford*), invalidating the Missouri Compromise and holding that Congress lacked authority to abolish slavery in the territories. That notorious decision, a step on the road to the Civil War, was perhaps not the best advertisement for judicial review. But since then, the Court has lost its early reticence. It has declared acts of Congress unconstitutional nearly 200 times.

How the modern Court exercises its great power—how cases reach the Court and how the justices proceed to select them and decide them—who the justices are and how they are chosen—are the subjects of the remainder of this book.

Chapter 2
The Court at work (1)

A disappointed litigant's vow to "take my case all the way to the Supreme Court!" is likely to prove an empty threat. An appeal on the way to the Supreme Court encounters many obstacles. Some derive from the Constitution itself; Article III limits the jurisdiction of the federal courts to deciding "cases" and "controversies," although, as we shall see, the meaning of those words is hardly self-evident. Another obstacle is inherent in the Supreme Court's place in the federal system: the Court generally may not review a state supreme court's interpretation of a state's own constitution. For example, the Court could not have reviewed the Massachusetts Supreme Judicial Court's decision in 2003 to grant same-sex couples the right to marry under state law—twelve years before the U.S. Supreme Court found the same right in the U.S. Constitution in *Obergefell v. Hodges*—because the state court based its decision on its interpretation of the Massachusetts Constitution (*Goodridge v. Department of Public Health*). (State high court decisions that interpret the U.S. Constitution do fall within the Supreme Court's jurisdiction, however.) Other obstacles to Supreme Court review stem from federal law. For example, Congress has set strict deadlines for filing Supreme Court appeals.

Someone who has followed all the rules and whose case falls cleanly within the Court's jurisdiction then encounters perhaps the most daunting obstacle of all: the justices' freedom to say no.

Unlike most appellate courts, which must act on all properly presented appeals, the Supreme Court has nearly complete control over its docket. Year in and year out, the justices agree to decide only about 1 percent of the cases that reach them. The Court hears appeals from the thirteen federal appeals courts, the high courts of the fifty states, and occasionally from other courts, including the highest court in the military justice system, the United States Court of Appeals for the Armed Forces. A small category of cases, most notably appeals concerning voting rights and redistricting, reach the Court directly from special federal district courts. During the 2018–19 term, 6,442 new petitions for review reached the Court. Carrying over 1,184 petitions from the previous term, including 38 that the justices had already agreed to hear but that had not yet been argued, the Court granted an additional 86 cases and issued a total of 66 opinions.

Several recent examples illustrate the types of cases the Supreme Court decides and how the justices approach the task of decision. While there is no typical Supreme Court case, there is a typical *range* of cases during a given term, with the cases that the Court has chosen to review falling roughly evenly into two main categories. One category consists of cases of constitutional interpretation, usually involving a claim that a federal or state statute or policy violates a provision of the Constitution. The second category consists of cases requiring the justices to decide the meaning or application of a federal statute. A subset of this category consists of cases about the work of federal agencies. (A third category consists of suits between states—the one or two cases every year that fall within the Court's "original jurisdiction" to hear such disputes. These are often new chapters in long-running disagreements over state boundaries or interstate water rights. The Court appoints a lawyer or retired judge as a "special master" to take evidence and make a recommendation. The process can take years.)

Constitutional cases

Some constitutional cases present structural issues involving the separation of powers. Is each branch exercising its allotted authority? Does Congress, or the president, have the authority to do what each seeks to do? Some recent examples: Did Congress have the power, under its constitutional authority to regulate interstate commerce, to require individuals to purchase health insurance (the so-called individual mandate under "Obamacare")? The Court said no in *National Federation of Independent Business v. Sebelius* (2012). But at the same time, in the same decision, the Court ruled that under its power to impose taxes, Congress could exact a penalty from taxpayers who failed to buy insurance, so the constitutional attack on the Affordable Care Act failed. Did the president have the unilateral authority to restrict entry into the country by residents of predominantly Muslim nations? The Court said yes in *Trump v. Hawaii* (2018).

More often, constitutional cases present claims of individual rights: free speech under the First Amendment, freedom from unreasonable search and seizure under the Fourth Amendment, a claim that a law or policy amounts to the denial of equal protection under the Fourteenth Amendment. Does a state-owned law school violate the equal-protection rights of white applicants by maintaining an admissions policy that favors minority applicants? (The Court said no in *Grutter v. Bollinger* (2003), on the ground that the policy served the state's "compelling interest" in increasing educational diversity. In *Fisher v. University of Texas* (2013), the Court gave the same answer in rejecting a challenge to another state's different approach to increasing diversity at its flagship university.) Do individuals have a measure of privacy with regard to their cell phones such that police ordinarily need a warrant to search a cell phone they find in a suspect's possession during an arrest? The Court said yes in *Riley v. California* (2014).

There are several observations to make about the Court's constitutional cases. First, only one of the cases mentioned here (the cell phone case) was decided unanimously; the rest garnered from one to four dissenting votes. So whatever the Constitution was saying, the justices acted on different understandings of its commands, an indication that the art of constitutional interpretation is far from a paint-by-numbers exercise. Second, many constitutional cases, like the affirmative-action case, require the justices to balance competing interests, in both instances a white plaintiff's claim of a right to equal treatment versus the state's assertion of society's need for an ethnically diverse educated population. Different justices will balance competing claims differently, in a context-laden process that is considerably more complex than simply deciding in a vacuum whether one side's claim is valid. Much of constitutional law, as it has evolved, entails some sort of balancing test between competing constitutional values.

Third, unlike the early justices, justices of the modern Court rarely find themselves in the position of confronting the Constitution head-on. Rather, constitutional questions reach the Court encrusted by layers of precedent built up over more than two centuries. Sometimes, of course, the decision is to reject the precedent: *Brown v. Board of Education* (1954) interpreted the Fourteenth Amendment's equal protection guarantee to prohibit official segregation, which a fifty-eight-year-old precedent, *Plessy v. Ferguson* (1896), had deemed acceptable as long as the "separate" facilities were "equal." But in the great majority of cases, the justices sift through the available precedents like miners panning for gold, hoping to find one that suggests an answer to the question at hand. Supreme Court opinions are not built from scratch. Most contain multiple quotations from the Court's earlier cases, from which the opinion writer reasons by analogy. In any area of doctrine in which the Court has been active for a long time, there are usually precedents that can plausibly support a variety of outcomes.

A case the Court decided in 2008 was a rare exception. Surprisingly enough, the Court had never issued an authoritative interpretation of the Second Amendment's reference to "the right of the people to keep and bear arms," so there was no binding law to apply to the question of whether the District of Columbia's prohibition on individual handgun ownership was constitutional. There was, of course, the amendment's opaque, one-sentence text: "A well regulated militia, being necessary to the security of a free state, the right of the people to keep and bear arms, shall not be infringed." Even leaving aside the excessive punctuation, the sentence is confusing, and its implications for individual gun rights, divorced from the context of a "well-regulated militia," are unclear. In *District of Columbia v. Heller*, Justice Antonin Scalia, for the five-member majority, and Justice John Paul Stevens, for the four dissenters, grappled with the text and history of the Second Amendment and reached opposite conclusions. Who were "the people" whose right the amendment was protecting? According to Justice Scalia, these were the same "people" who enjoyed the other individual rights protected by the Bill of Rights, such as the First Amendment's "right of the people peaceably to assemble." The amendment codified a "pre-existing" individual right to self-defense, Scalia concluded. But to Justice Stevens, "the people" addressed by the Second Amendment were those with a duty to serve in the state militia, and the right was a collective one, to be exercised only in connection with military service. The two sides also disagreed over what the amendment implied by the words "bear arms." Justice Stevens regarded the phrase as an idiom limited to the context of military service. Justice Scalia, recognizing no such limitation, interpreted the phrase as referring more generally to self-defense.

One of the four dissenters, Justice Stephen G. Breyer, while signing the Stevens dissent, proposed an alternative approach, which he called a "focus on practicalities." The question he asked was what purpose the District of Columbia's statute served and how that purpose might relate to the interests the Framers of the

Second Amendment sought to protect. The District meant to protect public safety in a densely populated urban environment, Justice Breyer observed. He noted that during the colonial period, the major cities of the American colonies pursued a similar goal by restricting the storage of gunpowder in private homes, where it presented a fire hazard. Boston flatly prohibited bringing loaded firearms into "any dwelling-house" or "other building, within the Town of Boston," despite a provision in the Massachusetts Constitution that granted "the people...a right to keep and to bear arms for the common defence." Breyer's conclusion was that even if the Second Amendment was understood to protect an individual right, the Framers contemplated exceptions, and the District's gun-control law was compatible with the original understanding.

As the Second Amendment example shows, justices employ a variety of tools to interpret the Constitution. Text and history are the commonly accepted starting points although, as this case demonstrates, neither may provide a definitive answer. In his 1997 book, *A Matter of Interpretation: Federal Courts and the Law,* Justice Scalia (who died in 2016) described himself as a textualist and an "originalist" who believed that the only legitimate basis for interpreting a provision of the Constitution is the original understanding of the Constitution's Framers. "If the courts are free to write the Constitution anew," he warned, "they will, by God, write it the way the majority wants...By trying to make the Constitution do everything that needs doing from age to age, we shall have caused it to do nothing at all."

Justice Breyer, on the other hand, advocates a "pragmatic" approach that rejects overarching theories in favor of "a Constitution that works well for the people today." In his own book on constitutional interpretation, *Making Our Democracy Work: A Judge's View* (2010), Breyer writes that "the Court should reject approaches to interpreting the Constitution that consider the document's scope and application as fixed at the moment of framing. Rather, the Court should regard the Constitution as containing unwavering values that must be applied flexibly to ever-changing circumstances."

Statutory cases

Although at first glance cases that require the justices to interpret statutes might seem simpler, the statutory side of the Court's docket presents many of the same challenges and has provoked similar disputes over basic principles of interpretation.

If a statute was perfectly clear, chances are that it would not be the subject of a Supreme Court case. But it is the rare statute that by its own terms answers every question that might arise. Perhaps Congress failed to anticipate the full range of situations in which the statute might be invoked. Or, quite often, the task of addressing all the possible applications of a bill under consideration exceeds the legislative appetite for detail or requires one compromise too many. Congress is then quite happy to let the courts fill in the blanks. After all, unlike a constitutional ruling, a ruling on the meaning of a statute can be overturned by new legislation if Congress concludes that the courts have come up with the wrong answer.

The Americans with Disabilities Act provides a vivid example. Since its enactment in 1990, this major civil rights law, which prohibits discrimination on the basis of disability, has been the subject of dozens of court decisions, including several major Supreme Court rulings. The law's prohibitions are, for the most part, clear, but what is a disability? Congress provided only a spare definition: "(A) a physical or mental impairment that substantially limits one or more of the major life activities; (B) a record of such an impairment; or (C) being regarded as having such an impairment." The Equal Employment Opportunity Commission, the federal agency charged with administering the law, in turn issued a regulation defining "major life activities" to include "functions such as caring for oneself, performing manual tasks, walking, seeing, hearing, speaking, breathing, learning, and working."

A question arose quickly: What if someone had a condition that met one of the definitions but that could be mitigated by medication or by a medical device? Did the person still have a disability within the meaning of the law? Which counted, the corrected state or the uncorrected state? The statute and the regulations were silent. Two women with poor but completely correctable eyesight brought a lawsuit under the act after they were turned down for jobs as airline pilots. They argued that since they had been denied employment on the basis of their eyesight, they should be considered disabled and protected against employment discrimination. The Supreme Court found otherwise in *Sutton v. United Airlines* (1999), noting that with glasses, the women were not limited in any major life activity. Congress intended to limit the law's coverage "to only those whose impairments are not mitigated by corrective measures," the Court concluded. A man whose high blood pressure was controlled by medication was fired from his job as a commercial truck driver when the employer learned of his hypertension diagnosis. He sued, arguing that the law protected him. In *Murphy v. United Parcel Service* (1999), the Supreme Court rejected the claim, on the same ground: when medicated, the truck driver was not limited in a major life activity. Finally, confronted with a tide of individual claims, the Court attempted a more general clarification. In *Toyota Motor Mfg. v. Williams* (2002), the justices rejected the claim of a woman who was unable to continue in her assembly-line job because carpal-tunnel syndrome limited her ability to perform the required manual tasks. The Court held that "the central inquiry must be whether the claimant is unable to perform the variety of tasks central to most people's daily lives, not whether the claimant is unable to perform the tasks associated with her specific job."

It is worth noting that the first two decisions were not unanimous. Two justices, Stevens and Breyer, objected in dissent, in the case of the nearsighted pilots, that the Court had reached the "counterintuitive conclusion" that the law's "safeguards vanish when individuals make themselves more employable by ascertaining ways to overcome their physical or mental limitations." Observing that the Americans with Disabilities Act was designed to redress a common cause of discrimination, the two justices said that rather than read the law narrowly, the Court should follow "a familiar canon of statutory construction that remedial legislation should be construed broadly to effectuate its purposes."

One other anti-discrimination statute deserves mention here: the Pregnancy Discrimination Act, which Congress passed in 1978 to protect pregnant women from discrimination on the job. The question confronting the Court in a 2015 case, *Young v. United Parcel Service, Inc.*, was whether the law entitled a pregnant UPS driver to a temporary accommodation due to her doctor's orders not to lift more than ten pounds for the duration of her pregnancy. Drivers were ordinarily expected to be able to lift up to seventy pounds. UPS provided temporary light duty for drivers injured on the job, but not for those with non-job-related injuries. The Pregnancy Discrimination Act provides that "women affected by pregnancy" must be "treated the same" as "other persons not so affected but similar in the ability or inability to work." In which category did the plaintiff in this case fit? She had clearly not been injured on the job, but if she was simply placed in the category of all other drivers with temporary disabilities, she would have no claim, and a law intended to protect pregnant women would mean very little. The plaintiff, Peggy Young, had lost in the lower courts. The Supreme Court, voting six to three, sent the case back for reconsideration after describing a pathway by which Ms. Young could show that the company's policy was so unnecessarily burdensome on pregnant workers as to amount to illegal discrimination. (The case settled without further legal proceedings; UPS, in the meantime, had changed its policy to grant pregnant employees in the future the accommodation that Ms. Young had sought.)

The disability cases illustrate conflicting approaches to the task of statutory interpretation: one, an effort to fit the case at hand to the statute's precise words, and the other, an effort to step back and interpret the statute in light of the congressional purpose in enacting it. To ascertain purpose often requires reference to the statute's legislative history—to the floor debates, the records of committee hearings, committee reports, and the final reports of the Senate and House of Representatives. For the disability act, as the dissenters pointed out, these materials made it clear that whether a person had a disability was to be determined based on the person's uncorrected state; a person with hearing loss, for example, was to be deemed limited in the major life activity of hearing without regard to whether hearing aids could correct the problem.

Justice Breyer has argued that courts, as "partners in the enterprise," should use the materials at hand to help Congress carry out its legislative purposes. Justice Scalia, by contrast, refused to cite legislative history at all, due to what he considers its unreliability and "manipulability" by congressional staff members. Rather than guess at an underlying purpose, he argued, courts should simply hold Congress to the precise language that it enacts into law. He was a powerful presence at the Court during his thirty-year tenure, and his war against legislative history made many of his colleagues, even those who disagreed with him on this point, shy away from citing it in their opinions. That is not to say that they did not consider legislative history to be an informative tool at least some of the time.

Administrative agencies

The steady growth of the administrative state means that the Supreme Court is often presented with the question of whether an administrative agency is properly carrying out its assigned duties. Notable cases in recent years have been driven by disputes over environmental policy and the enforcement, or lack of enforcement, of the nation's environmental laws. Although the Clean Air Act and the Clear Water Act are decades old, dating to the 1970s, disputes over these statutes continue to provide the Court with a steady diet of cases.

If the statute governing an agency is unclear as to the matter at hand, the Court will defer to the agency's plausible interpretation of its mandate. But if the statute is unambiguous, the Court directs the agency to carry out the will of Congress.

The refusal of the Environmental Protection Agency to regulate motor vehicle emissions of carbon dioxide and three other heat-trapping gasses presented such a case late in the administration of President George W. Bush. The agency had turned down a petition from a coalition of environmental groups requesting it to initiate a formal rule-making process leading to the regulation of "tailpipe emissions" associated with climate change. In refusing to act, the EPA said it lacked authority under the Clean Air Act because the so-called greenhouse gasses were not "air pollutants" within the meaning of the statute. In an appeal brought by Massachusetts, other states, and a group of environmental organizations, the Court disagreed, noting that the Clean Air act was "unambiguous" in including these gasses within its "sweeping definition" of "air pollutants." Going forward, the Court said in *Massachusetts v. Environmental Protection Agency* (2007), the agency could refuse to regulate only if it could provide a reason for doing so based on science, not policy.

This case was notable for another dimension beyond administrative law. Four justices argued in dissent that the Court lacked authority to decide the case because the agency's challengers did not have "standing"; they could not show, the dissenters said, that they suffered any actual injury from the refusal to regulate. Thus according to the dissent, the dispute was not the kind of "case" or "controversy" that met the Article III requirements for jurisdiction.

Consideration of this argument brings us back to a discussion of the obstacles to jurisdiction in the Supreme Court and the other federal courts. The Court has spent many years interpreting the words "cases" and "controversies." From the beginning, the Court has refused to offer advisory opinions. There must be a concrete dispute between adversarial parties, one that is ripe for adjudication and not rendered moot by some intervening event. Essential to meeting the case-and-controversy requirement is a plaintiff with standing, a concept with three elements. First, the party bringing the suit must have suffered an injury that is actual or imminent—that is, not hypothetical—and particularized—that is, personal and not shared with the population as a whole. (This requirement eliminates most forms of "taxpayer standing"; members of the public do not have a right, simply by virtue of their status as taxpayers, to go to court to challenge policies they disagree with or believe to be unconstitutional.) Second, the plaintiff must show that the defendant caused the injury by an unlawful action or failure to act. Third, the injury must be of a sort for which a court can actually grant relief. These three requirements are often boiled down to the shorthand: "injury-in-fact, causation, and redressability."

The majority in the Environmental Protection Agency case found that at least one of the multiple plaintiffs, Massachusetts, met all three requirements. The state faced losing coastal land to rising seas ("injury-in-fact") in a process due at least incrementally to the contribution that emissions from motor vehicles were making to global warming ("causation"). And regulation by the agency to reduce the emissions would at least to some degree mitigate the problem ("redressability"). The dissenters argued that the state met none of the requirements: that its assertion of injury was conjectural, not sufficiently traceable to the agency's inaction, and insufficiently likely to be redressed by regulation. The lawsuit, the dissenters concluded, did not meet the case-or-controversy requirement of Article III.

Clearly, jurisdictional issues such as these are contested territory in the modern Supreme Court. As this case demonstrates, each jurisdictional requirement is open to interpretation. The concepts at issue are not static. The Court's willingness to find standing has expanded and contracted over time, often reflecting how closely the justices care to scrutinize the activity of the other branches of government. Jurisdictional questions may appear technical and arcane, but they provide an indispensable window into how the justices see the Court's role at a given point in time.

One final observation: since the Court operates by majority rule, justices are effective at projecting their personal views only to the extent that they can persuade others. That is not to say that individual views are unimportant. On a closely divided Court, a justice can withhold a vote from one group and cost that side a majority. But to shape the law affirmatively, a justice needs allies, usually four of them. Further, the norm of adjudication requires giving reasons. A Supreme Court opinion typically describes the facts of the case and the range of relevant precedents and legal principles, and then gives the reasons why one legal path rather than another leads to the correct resolution. Any of those steps—fitting the facts together, describing the relevant law, and choosing a path to the final judgment—may be contested in a given case, and a justice writing a majority opinion must persuade a majority of all three if the opinion is actually to speak for "the Court."

Chapter 3
The justices

There are no formal requirements for becoming a Supreme Court justice. The Constitution requires a senator to have reached the age of thirty, and a president to be at least thirty-five and a "natural born citizen," but it sets no comparable rules for justices. Theoretically, anyone who can get nominated by the president and confirmed by a majority vote of the Senate can be a Supreme Court justice. Everyone who has served on the Court has been a lawyer, however, although many of the early justices were not law school graduates; as was customary, they had "read law" under the supervision of a member of the bar. (The last justice without a formal legal education was Robert H. Jackson, who joined the Court in 1941; he had been admitted to the New York bar after only one year of law school.)

After setting the membership of the Supreme Court at six (one chief and five associate justices) in the first Judiciary Act, Congress proceeded to change the number of justices five times: to seven in 1807, nine in 1837, ten in 1863 (the tenth seat was never filled), and seven again in 1866 before settling at the present nine in 1869. While perceptions of the Court's workload played a role in the variable number of seats, so did politics: the 1866 elimination of two seats effectively prevented President Andrew Johnson from making any Supreme Court appointments, while the increase to nine after the election of President Ulysses S. Grant gave the new president two new seats to fill. In 1937 Congress rejected President Franklin D. Roosevelt's proposal to add a new justice, up to a total of fifteen, any time an incumbent reached the age of seventy and refused to retire. While it is unlikely that the size of the Court will ever change again, some scholars, troubled by the increasing length of service on the Court and the advanced age at which justices retire, have recently put forward a proposal that would add new justices, move the oldest into a senior status, and assign the Court's active work to the most junior nine. More recently, progressive advocates who were enraged by the Senate Republicans' refusal even to meet with President Obama's 2016 Supreme Court nominee, Chief Judge Merrick Garland, have argued that increasing the Court by a justice or two would be only fair. The notion of term limits for the Supreme Court has also come in for renewed attention.

Initially, the Court's membership was entirely Protestant as well as, needless to say, white and male. The first Roman Catholic on the Court was the fifth chief justice, Roger B. Taney, appointed in 1836. Not until Thurgood Marshall's appointment in 1967 was the Court's membership anything other than all white, and not until Sandra Day O'Connor joined the Court in 1981 was it anything other than all male. Since then, the Court has slowly come to reflect more of the nation's diversity, although the reflection is not without distortions. On Thurgood Marshall's retirement in 1991, his seat was filled by a second African American, Clarence Thomas. Ruth Bader Ginsburg joined O'Connor on the bench in 1993. The Court that convened on October 4, 2010, for the start of its new term included, for the first time, three women (Ginsburg, Sonia Sotomayor, and Elena Kagan); one African American, Thomas; one Latina, Sotomayor; six Catholics; and three Jews. John Paul Stevens was the only Protestant on the Court when he retired in 2010. The nomination of the first Jewish justice, Louis D. Brandeis in 1916, had stirred controversy, and for many years there was a sole "Jewish seat" on the Court. But by the time Elena Kagan joined the Court in 2010 as one of three Jewish

justices (with Ginsburg and Breyer), a nominee's religious
background no longer received much public attention.

A justice's place of origin has also faded in relevance. For many
years, presidents had tried to achieve some geographic balance on
the Court, reflecting the notion that different regions of the
country had different interests and perspectives that the Court
should reflect. But geography evidently no longer mattered by the
time Kagan joined the Court as a fourth New Yorker (with Scalia,
Ginsburg, and Sotomayor). Neighboring New Jersey produced a
fifth justice, Samuel A. Alito Jr.

The modern Court has also notably lacked diversity of professional
background. Following Sandra Day O'Connor's retirement in

3. The first four women ever to serve on the Supreme Court gather at
the Court for Justice Elena Kagan's investiture, October 1, 2010. From
left, retired Justice Sandra Day O'Connor, Justice Sonia Sotomayor,
Justice Ruth Bader Ginsburg, and Justice Elena Kagan.

2006 and her replacement by Alito, all the members of the Court, for the first time in the country's history, had been federal appeals court judges immediately before their appointments. Elena Kagan's nomination in 2010 broke that mold. Solicitor general of the United States and before that, dean of Harvard Law School, she was the first Supreme Court nominee in thirty-nine years (since the 1971 nominations of William H. Rehnquist and Lewis F. Powell Jr.) never to have been a judge. President Trump's nominees, Neil M. Gorsuch, Brett M. Kavanaugh, and Amy Coney Barrett, were all judges on federal appeals courts at the time of their nominations.

Few would have predicted such resumé-narrowing back in earlier days, when justices were drawn from the top ranks of the executive and legislative branches. Members of the Warren Court (1953–69), for example, included three former United States senators (Hugo L. Black, Harold H. Burton, and Sherman Minton, only one of whom, Minton, had prior judicial service). Two others had been attorney general of the United States (Robert H. Jackson and Tom C. Clark, neither of whom had been judges). Others had held elective office at the local, state, or federal level. Chief Justice Earl Warren himself had served three terms as governor of California and had run for vice president on the national Republican ticket in 1948. He had never been a judge.

The change in the biography deemed appropriate for members of the Supreme Court is due in significant measure to the politics of the modern nomination and confirmation process. More than in the past, that process has become an occasion for a national debate about the role of the Court and the constitutional values that justices should be expected to uphold. Of course there has always been political conflict surrounding Supreme Court nominations, as presidents since George Washington have learned and as Franklin D. Roosevelt's effort to tame a recalcitrant Supreme Court exemplifies. But recent decades of divided government, increasing partisanship in Congress, the Court's high visibility in debates over divisive social issues plus its own close ideological balance have combined to raise the stakes for any nomination. Add the ability of partisans to conduct saturation-level media campaigns and it is easy to understand that a president faced with filling a Supreme Court vacancy wants no surprises, either in the confirmation process or during the nominee's subsequent service on the Court. The most readily available insurance policy against the unknown, although obviously far from perfect, is a judicial record that indicates how a potential nominee approaches the craft of judging as well as specific legal issues. In fact, appointing a sitting judge can serve a dual purpose for the president by providing a recognized credential the president can point to in order to buffer any implication that the selection was driven by ideology.

Nonetheless, a president who seeks to use a Supreme Court appointment to advance an agenda that Congress has not embraced, especially when the balance on the Court is perceived to be at stake, is most likely to meet resistance no matter how impressive the credentials of the nominee. The battle over President Ronald Reagan's nomination of Judge Robert H. Bork in 1987 is often depicted as the event that created the modern "confirmation mess." Although perhaps different only in degree rather than in kind, the Bork battle was a politically galvanizing event that played out in a bright media spotlight and left a legacy of bitterness that shaped the handling of subsequent nominations.

The Bork nomination had every ingredient of a recipe for political conflagration. The Reagan administration, having lost the Senate to the Democrats the previous November, was in a weakened political position, vexed by the Iran-Contra foreign policy scandal. Judge Bork, a longtime law professor whom the administration had placed on a federal appeals court to ready him for a Supreme Court nomination, was an outspoken conservative with a long list of publications arguing against the tenets of modern constitutional law. Lewis Powell, the moderate conservative Bork was named to replace, was the "swing" justice of his day, holding the balance of power on a closely divided Court, so that a potential Justice Bork was seen as an agent of change on such issues as abortion and affirmative action, both of which Powell had supported to at least some degree.

A coalition of liberal groups and leading Democratic senators organized to defeat the nomination by depicting Bork as "out of the mainstream." The nominee played into his opponents' hands during a week of televised testimony before the Senate Judiciary Committee, during which he defended his "originalist" judicial philosophy and offered gruff criticism of the Court's reliance on a right to privacy, not found in the Constitution's text, to protect a couple's right to use contraception and a woman's right to abortion. There is little doubt that the defeat of Robert Bork's nomination, by a vote of 58 against to 42 in favor, staved off a sharply conservative turn on the Court. A centrist conservative, Anthony M. Kennedy, a judge on the federal appeals court in California, was ultimately confirmed to the seat. He supported the right to abortion and, in equally sharp contrast with Bork, embraced a robust view of the First Amendment right to free speech. During the years following the terrorist attacks of September 11, 2001, Kennedy voted repeatedly with the Court's majority to reject President Bush's claim of unilateral authority over detention policies for enemy fighters. Robert Bork, from the sidelines, denounced those decisions.

There has been an intermittent debate over the years over whether the Senate should defer to the President's Supreme Court choices if the nominees' professional qualifications were satisfactory, without regard to senators' own ideological preferences. As a theoretical matter, that debate may be still ongoing in some quarters. As a practical matter, the Bork battle resolved it. The Senate asserted the right to evaluate qualifications, which Judge Bork certainly possessed, through the lens of ideology, which in his case alarmed a majority of the senators. "Judge Bork's confined vision of the Constitution and of the task of judging itself carries too great a risk of disservice to future national needs and distortion of age-old constitutional commitments to permit his confirmation," the Judiciary Committee's report on the nomination concluded after reviewing Bork's testimony for nearly one hundred pages.

After Bork's defeat, his supporters warned that presidents would never again be able to put forward a nominee who had accumulated a "paper trail" of engagement with the great issues of the day. That prediction did not prove precisely accurate. Before becoming a federal appeals court judge, Ruth Bader Ginsburg had been a leading civil rights lawyer who, in a half dozen Supreme Court arguments during the 1970s, played a major role in persuading the justices to regard sex discrimination as a matter of constitutional concern. Her record of advocacy, her paper trail, was long. Yet she was quickly and easily confirmed, by a vote of 96 to 3. One difference was that both the White House and the Senate were in Democratic hands. Another was that in twelve years on the appeals court (overlapping with Robert Bork's brief service on the same court), she had shown herself to be a cautious, centrist-minded judge. Further, the positions for which she had advocated had for the most part been adopted by the Supreme Court and could not plausibly be described as "out of the mainstream."

Yet despite coming before the Judiciary Committee in a position of strength in 1993, Ginsburg set a precedent that shaped subsequent confirmation hearings: she declined to engage the senators in more than minimal conversation about her views. Without disavowing any of her public positions, she refused to answer abstract questions and deflected more specific questions by saying that she should not take a position on an issue that might well come before the Court. Later nominees also took refuge in this strategy, with the result that the modern confirmation hearing has become a largely unrevealing ritual.

(Ginsburg's appeals court colleague, Antonin Scalia, had in fact employed an extreme version of the say-nothing strategy at his Supreme Court confirmation hearing in 1986, telling the senators that "I do not think I should answer any questions regarding any specific Supreme Court opinion, even one as fundamental as *Marbury v. Madison*.")

John Roberts, nominated by President George W. Bush to be chief justice in 2005, also had a paper trail, one of memos and analyses he had written as a young lawyer in the Justice Department and White House during the Reagan administration. Some were dismissive of civil rights claims and many were unmistakably conservative in tone. But Roberts—also a judge on the same appeals court where Bork and Ginsburg had served—came to his confirmation hearing prepared to deflect questions about his views. Unlike policymakers, Roberts said in his opening statement, judges are bound by precedent and should approach their role with "a certain humility." He told the senators: "Judges are like umpires. Umpires don't make the rules; they apply them." Not all senators were reassured, but enough were. The senate confirmed the seventeenth chief justice by a vote of 78 to 22, with the "no" votes coming from half the chamber's forty-four Democrats. Samuel A. Alito Jr., a conservative appeals court judge nominated by President Bush to succeed Justice O'Connor, faced an even more divided Senate. He was confirmed in January 2006 by a vote of 58 to 42, with only four Democrats voting in favor.

Clearly, something was changing in the politics of Supreme Court nominations and confirmations. As recently as the confirmations of Justices Ginsburg and Breyer, both nominated by President Bill Clinton, the lesson of the post-Bork era had appeared to be that a president who chose a Supreme Court nominee from the current ideological mainstream would face little difficulty in getting that nominee confirmed with broad bipartisan support; Ginsburg was confirmed in 1993 by a vote of 96 to 3 and Breyer was confirmed the next year by a vote of 87 to 9.

But by the time the next nominees of a Democratic president faced the Senate, partisanship had taken over. President Barack Obama had reason to suppose that his two nominees, Sonia Sotomayor to succeed Justice Souter in 2009 and Elena Kagan to succeed Justice Stevens in 2010, would face little opposition in the Democratic-controlled Senate. Not only were they well qualified by conventional criteria—Sotomayor had spent seventeen years as a federal judge and Kagan, the first woman to be dean of Harvard Law School, was at the time serving as solicitor general of the United States—but their presence on the Court was not expected to shift the ideological balance. But the Senate majority leader, Mitch McConnell of Kentucky, called on his fellow Republicans to make the vote a test of party loyalty. Only nine Republicans voted to confirm Sotomayor, who won confirmation by a vote of 68 to 31, and only five voted in favor of Kagan, who was confirmed by a vote of 63 to 37.

It was a taste of things to come. Hours after Justice Scalia's unexpected death in February 2016, at the age of seventy-nine, Senator McConnell, now the majority leader, surprised the country by announcing that because it was an election year, the Senate would not confirm anyone President Obama nominated. The next president should fill the vacancy, McConnell maintained. Consequently, Merrick Garland, the highly respected chief judge of the federal appeals court in Washington, DC, never got a hearing before the Senate Judiciary Committee; most Republican senators refused to meet with him. By making it clear that not only the White House but also the Supreme Court was at stake in the November election, McConnell succeeded in motivating the Republican base. Some analysts have credited the strategy with contributing to Donald Trump's victory.

Eleven days after his inauguration, President Trump nominated Neil M. Gorsuch, a forty-nine-year-old federal appeals court judge from Denver. When the Senate Democrats, who regarded the seat as "stolen," threatened to filibuster the nomination, Senator

McConnell led the Republicans in changing the Senate's rules. No longer would sixty votes be necessary to close debate and end a filibuster. A bare majority of fifty-one votes would suffice. Gorsuch was confirmed by a vote of 54 to 45, with three Democratic senators voting for confirmation.

In 2018, following Justice Kennedy's retirement, President Trump nominated Judge Brett M. Kavanaugh of the federal appeals court in Washington, DC. Because Justice Kennedy sat at the ideological center of the Court and Judge Kavanaugh appeared well to his right, a confirmation battle was assured. Kavanaugh's confirmation became even more contentious when a woman he had known as a teenager testified that he had sexually assaulted her during a high school party decades earlier. Kavanaugh angrily denied the charge. The episode played out as a television drama reminiscent of the confrontation between Clarence Thomas and Anita Hill before the Senate Judiciary Committee in 1991. The nomination survived the controversy, but barely. Kavanaugh was confirmed by a vote of 51 to 49, with one Democrat voting in favor and one Republican voting against.

Although Senator McConnell had insisted in 2016 that the Senate should not fill a Supreme Court vacancy during a presidential election year, he quickly abandoned that policy when Justice Ruth Bader Ginsburg died on September 18, 2020, just six weeks before Election Day. On September 26, with Justice Ginsburg's empty chair in the courtroom still draped in black, President Trump nominated Judge Amy Coney Barrett, a former law professor whom he had named three years earlier to the federal appeals court in Chicago. Democrats were outraged by the speed of the nomination and the rushed confirmation hearing that promptly followed. They boycotted much of the hearing and did not give Judge Barrett a single vote for confirmation. Justice Barrett took her seat on October 27, in time for the new term's second round or arguments – which, due to the COVID-19 pandemic, the justices conducted over the telephone, with the audio streamed to the public.

Despite the attention that presidents and senators pay to Supreme Court nominations, nominees do not always turn out as forecast. Political scientists have charted the phenomenon of "ideological drift" and have concluded that it is common—even, perhaps, the rule rather than the exception, with some justices shifting ideological direction more than once. The leading example in recent decades is that of Harry A. Blackmun, appointed in 1970 by President Richard Nixon as a reliable conservative who gave every sign of being an ideological soul mate of his boyhood friend, the recently appointed chief justice Warren E. Burger. Yet by the time Blackmun retired twenty-four years later, he was the most liberal member of the Court—to be sure, a more conservative Court than the one he had joined, but his leftward migration on nearly all important issues was striking. John Paul Stevens, another Republican appointee, became more liberal during his tenure of more than thirty-four years. To a lesser degree, so did Sandra Day O'Connor and David H. Souter, likewise Republican appointees. The category of justices who became more conservative while on the Court appears much smaller. That is perhaps because no Democratic president made a Supreme Court nomination from 1967 until 1993, leaving a very small pool of justices who might be in a position to drift to the right. Arguably the most recent to have done so was Byron R. White, appointed in 1962 by President John F. Kennedy.

How can substantial changes in outlook be explained among a group of mature, professionally experienced individuals? (Blackmun was sixty-one when he was named to the Court, and had been a federal appeals court judge for eleven years.) Robert Jackson, observing the Court as FDR's attorney general, posed a version of that question in a book he published shortly before his own appointment as a justice in 1941. "Why is it," he asked in *The Struggle for Judicial Supremacy*, "that the Court influences appointees more consistently than appointees influence the Court?" Indeed, Jackson himself changed while on the Court: initially a strong supporter of presidential power, he grew skeptical of its exercise, and in 1952 wrote an opinion, still widely cited today, setting out a framework for confining a president's assertion of authority (*Youngstown Sheet & Tube Co. v. Sawyer*).

As Jackson's question suggests, the experience of serving on the Court is a unique and powerful one, providing new perspectives that can dislodge preconceived notions—for some, but obviously not for all. The author of a study of the twelve Republican-appointed justices between 1969 and 2006 found a strong correlation between prior service in the federal executive branch and ideological stability as a Supreme Court justice. Half of the group had held substantial executive branch positions before joining the Court while half had not. Only those without such experience drifted leftward. Another scholar, going back to Earl Warren's appointment in 1953, pointed to residency at the time of appointment as the distinguishing feature between those who exhibited "voting change" on civil liberties issues and those who did not. Those who were living in Washington, DC, at the time of their nomination tended not to change, while those who came to the Court from outside the Beltway became more liberal. Of course, there is substantial, although not complete, overlap between those with executive branch experience and those living in Washington. Perhaps the challenging experience of a midlife move to a new city makes a new justice even more open to new perceptions.

The Constitution makes federal judges, along with the president, vice president, and "all civil officers of the United States" subject to impeachment for "high crimes and misdemeanors." Although a dozen judges of the lower federal courts have been impeached by the House of Representatives, convicted by the Senate, and removed from office following criminal convictions, Congress has never removed a Supreme Court justice. The House voted in 1804 to impeach Justice Samuel Chase on charges of sedition. Chase was a fervent partisan of the former president, John Adams. He had angered the newly empowered Jeffersonian Republicans by his speeches and particularly by a grand jury charge he delivered as a circuit judge that criticized President Jefferson. Chase had, however, committed no crime, and the Senate acquitted him. He remained on the Court for another seven years. The episode established the principle that disagreement with a judge's judicial acts is not a valid reason for impeachment.

Nonetheless, there were calls during the 1960s for the impeachment of Chief Justice Earl Warren, and in 1970 the Republican leader of the House of Representatives, Gerald R. Ford, led an effort to impeach Justice William O. Douglas, an outspoken liberal. Ford's campaign against Douglas, backed by the Nixon administration, centered on the justice's activities off the bench, including his multiple marriages, publication of a book and magazine articles, and

4. William O. Douglas, photographed on March 20, 1939, the day of his nomination to the Supreme Court by President Franklin D. Roosevelt. Appointed at the age of forty, Douglas was the longest-serving justice in history, retiring in 1975 after thirty-six years.

service on the board of a private foundation. When asked to explain how these activities amounted to impeachable offenses, Ford replied that "an impeachable offense is whatever a majority of the House of Representatives considers it to be in a given moment of history." The House Judiciary Committee investigated the complaint against Douglas at length but declined to recommend impeachment, and the effort died. Douglas retired in 1975 after a tenure of thirty-six years, the longest in the Court's history. Through an odd twist of fate, Gerald Ford had become president a year earlier when Richard Nixon resigned in the face of impeachment.

Finally, another word about the question of life tenure. When the Constitution was being debated, life tenure for judges was not a given. Thomas Jefferson opposed it, arguing for renewable terms of four to six years. But the Framers chose to protect judicial independence by a guarantee of tenure "during good Behavior" as well as by providing that a judge's salary could not be reduced.

Today, however, criticism comes from both the Right and the Left, from scholars who argue that when justices linger well into advanced old age in order to time their retirements according to political loyalty, and when presidents try to project their legacies far into the future by seeking ever younger nominees, life tenure exerts a distorting effect on both the institutional life of the Supreme Court and the political life of the country. Certainly justices are living longer and staying longer. Between 1789 and 1970, justices served an average of fifteen years. It is now nearly twice that. The Court went without a vacancy for eleven years between 1994 and 2005, the longest period without turnover since the 1820s.

Removing life tenure directly would require a constitutional amendment, an arduous if not impossible task. So some advocates of change have proposed a statutory work-around that would achieve much the same result: continuing to appoint justices for life, but establishing that the term of active service would be eighteen years. A justice would then move into the semi-retired ranks, similar to the system in place for the lower federal courts, available to be called upon to break a tie when only eight justices would otherwise be available to sit, or for other judicial duties. The opening for a position as one of the nine active justices would then be taken by a new appointee. Under this system, a new justice would be appointed every two years. In other words, every president would get two appointments, thus regularizing the current randomness with which vacancies now occur. No president would have to suffer the drought that Jimmy Carter faced, without a single Supreme Court vacancy to fill during his presidency.

The critics of life tenure note that all other constitutional democracies, while borrowing much from the American example, including the norm of judicial independence, have rejected life tenure for their high court judges. Canada, Australia, Israel, and India, for example, impose fixed age limits, while the constitutional courts of Germany, France, and South Africa have fixed terms. Among the fifty states, only Rhode Island has placed no limits on the tenure of the judges on its state supreme court. The critique of life tenure may never gain public traction in the United States. But it poses the provocative question of where protection for judicial independence most reliably lies: on paper alone, or in a country's culture of learned expectations from courts that in turn preserve public trust with reasoned judgment.

Chapter 4
The chief justice

Article III, the judicial article of the Constitution, does not even bother to mention a chief justice. Clearly, the Framers intended there to be one, but we can derive that intention only by inference from the text of the Constitution itself—from the explicit requirement in Article I for the chief justice to preside over the Senate trial in any impeachment of a president. Chief Justice John G. Roberts Jr. filled that role during the Senate impeachment trial of President Donald Trump in early 2020. His predecessor, Chief Justice William H. Rehnquist, asked to describe his role in the 1999 impeachment trial of President Bill Clinton, replied with a smile: "I did nothing in particular, and I did it very well."

No matter what the Framers envisioned, no one would maintain today that the chief justice does nothing in particular. The office has grown enormously over the intervening centuries, both by statute and custom. A 2006 study compiled a list of eighty-one separate provisions by which Congress has conferred on the chief justice a specific duty or power. These range from directing the purchase of law books by the Library of Congress to appointing the eleven judges of the special court that authorizes the government to conduct foreign intelligence searches and wiretaps. The chief justice is, by law, a trustee of the National Gallery of Art and the Smithsonian Institution; presides over the Judicial Conference of the United States, which sets policy for the federal judiciary; and certifies the disability and eligibility for early retirement of another justice should that occasion arise.

The single most important power the chief justices exercise may still be to cast one of the nine votes that determine the outcome of a Supreme Court case. To the sixth chief justice, Salmon P. Chase, that was the only function that really mattered. "The extent of the power of the Chief Justice is vastly misconceived," Chase wrote in a letter in 1868. "In the Supreme Court he is but one of eight judges, each of whom has the same powers as himself. His judgment has no more weight, and his vote no more importance, than those of any of his brethren. He presides, and a good deal of extra labor is thrown upon him. That's all."

Even if the chief justice is simply first among equals on the bench, a twenty-first-century perspective on the job requires a broader appreciation of its power. It is more accurate to think of the chief justice today as a CEO, chief executive not only of the Supreme Court but of the entire judicial branch. The typical career path to the federal bench offers little preparation for such a multifaceted role. The best-prepared chief justice of the past century was undoubtedly William Howard Taft, the tenth chief justice, who had also been the twenty-seventh president. Taft, who served from 1921 to 1930, was, not surprisingly, one of the most effective chief justices.

Prior service on the Court is also useful preparation, although uncommon. Of the seventeen men who have served as chief justice, only four previously served as associate justices. Three—Rehnquist, Edward Douglass White, and Harlan Fiske Stone—received their promotions while they were sitting on the Court. (John Rutledge, George Washington's failed chief justice nominee, is not counted on this list because he never took the seat to which he had been confirmed as an associate justice.) The fourth former associate justice, Charles Evans Hughes, had resigned from the Court in order to run for president in 1916.

5. Chief Justice William Howard Taft, pictured at the start of his tenure in 1921. He is the only person to have served both as president and as a member of the Supreme Court.

Fourteen years later, on the death of Chief Justice Taft, President Herbert Hoover chose Hughes as the next chief justice.

Even if previously confirmed to the Court, a nominee for chief justice must receive a separate Senate confirmation and a new commission. As a matter of confirmation politics, that requirement perhaps serves as a disincentive for a president to elevate a sitting justice. As happened when President Reagan selected William Rehnquist for elevation in 1986, the confirmation process can easily turn into a referendum on the nominee's Supreme Court career so far, as well as on the direction of the Court as a whole.

The title we use today, Chief Justice of the United States, is obscure in origin. Neither the first Judiciary Act, nor the Constitution itself, says anything more elaborate than "chief justice." The unwieldy "Chief Justice of the Supreme Court of the United States" later came into use. In the 1860s, Congress began using the current title, which appeared on Melville W. Fuller's commission as chief justice in 1888.

Tradition, rather than statute, dictates much of how the chief justice operates in the job's purely judicial capacity. He runs "the Conference," the Court's word for the justices as a collective. When he has voted in the majority on a case, he exercises the prerogative of assigning either himself or one of the other justices in the majority to write the opinion. When the chief justice is in dissent, the senior justice in the majority makes the assignment.

The Court's practice is for the justices to write an approximately equal number of majority opinions over the course of the term. But the assignment function involves considerably more thought and strategy than simply going down a checklist. Just because five justices make up a majority to reverse or affirm a lower court decision does not mean that all five see the issues the same way or feel equally committed to the outcome or the rationale. So in a close case in which the majority's hold may be tenuous, it is rather common for the justice who is making the assignment—whether the chief justice or an associate—to give the writing assignment to the colleague whose commitment to the majority view appears the least firm. The expectation then is that the act of articulating the majority's reasons will persuade the wavering justice and forestall that most undesired outcome—defection by a justice who becomes persuaded that the dissent has the better of the argument.

That happens occasionally nonetheless. For example, the Court was closely divided during its 1991 term on the question of whether a prayer by a member of the clergy during a public high school's graduation exercise violated the constitutional separation of church and state. A federal appeals court had ruled that it did, and the Supreme Court agreed to hear the school district's appeal. After the argument, the justices voted 5 to 4 in *Lee v. Weisman* (1992) to reverse the lower court's decision and declare the clergy-led prayer constitutional. Chief Justice Rehnquist assigned the majority opinion to Justice Anthony M. Kennedy. While working on his opinion over the course of several months, Kennedy concluded that he was on the wrong side of the case—a conclusion that meant that the case would now come out the other way. Kennedy informed both the chief justice and Justice Harry A. Blackmun, who had been the senior associate justice on the dissenting side. "After writing to reverse in the high school graduation prayer case, my draft looked quite wrong," Kennedy informed Blackmun by letter, adding that he had rewritten his draft opinion to uphold the lower court's finding of unconstitutionality. The case was now Blackmun's to assign, and he told Kennedy to keep the assignment. Kennedy kept working, making some modifications to satisfy Blackmun and the other former dissenters. Several months later, in June 1992, the Court issued its 5-to-4 decision invalidating clergy-led prayer at public school graduation ceremonies. This behind-the-scenes drama remained unknown outside the Court for the next twelve years, until Justice

Blackmun's papers were opened to the public at the Library of Congress.

Control over the opinion assignments is an important source of power for the chief justice. Opinions can be written narrowly or broadly to reach the same result. A chief justice who wants to drive a doctrine in a certain direction, or keep an idea from gaining altitude, and who understands his colleague's styles and preferences can use the power to good effect. It is conventional for the chief justice, assuming that he is in the majority, to assign himself the opinion in cases with major political implications or in those that raise a serious issue of the allocation of power among the three branches of government. For example, Chief Justice Roberts wrote the majority opinion in *Trump v. Hawaii*, the case that upheld the president's ban on travel from Muslim countries. Chief Justice Burger's name is on the unanimous opinion in *United States v. Nixon*, the decision that required President Nixon to surrender the Watergate tapes and that led to the president's resignation in the face of impeachment. Still, at the end of the day, the chief justice, like the others, has only one vote.

Beyond managing the Court's judicial business, with the assistance of four law clerks, the chief justice is also in charge of a building where more than four hundred employees work. The Court has its own separate police force. It has a staff to manage a complex paper flow. Roughly 125 new appeals arrive every week, along with a steady flow of briefs in cases scheduled for argument. Each must be checked to ensure compliance with all the rules. Was the brief filed on time and within the word limit? Is its cover the right color? (The type of filing dictates the color of the cover, so that it can be seen at a glance whether the brief is a petition in a new case [white], a brief on the merits for the side defending the lower court's judgment [red], or a brief from a "friend of the court" [dark or light green, depending on which side the "friend" is supporting].) Sets of the filings for the week are placed on nine rolling carts for distribution to the justices' chambers. The Clerk of the Court (a senior official, not to be confused with a law clerk) supervises this process, while the Marshal is in charge of security. The chief justice also has an administrative assistant, known as counselor to the chief justice, who takes on significant duties both inside the building and outside, serving as the chief's liaison with agencies within the judicial branch.

One of these agencies is the Administrative Office of the United States Courts. As its name implies, the "A.O." is the federal judiciary's bureaucratic nerve center. The chief justice chooses the Administrative Office's director, who remains answerable to him. The federal court system, with 1,200 life-tenured judges, 850 other judges, 30,000 employees, and a budget of close to $6 billion, is itself a complex bureaucracy, and it is under the chief justice's ultimate supervision.

The chief justice also presides over the Judicial Conference of the United States, composed of the chief judges of each of the thirteen federal circuits plus an experienced district judge from each circuit, and the chief judge of the federal Court of International Trade. The Judicial Conference, which meets at the Supreme Court twice yearly, is a direct descendant of the Conference of Senior Circuit Judges, which Chief Justice Taft persuaded Congress to authorize. Its original purpose was to advise the chief justice "as to any matters in respect of which the administration of justice in the courts of the United States may be improved."

The Judicial Conference's mission today is a good deal broader. Much of its work is done in committees that propose the rules that govern important aspects of federal court jurisdiction and procedure. The twenty-two Judicial Conference committees have some 250 members, lawyers and judges who consider it an honor to be asked by the chief justice to serve. The conference itself communicates often with Congress on such matters as the need for additional judgeships or an increase in judicial pay. It comments as well on pending legislation that has a potential impact on the judiciary. In this capacity, both the Judicial Conference and the chief justice function as something close to lobbyists, seeking to achieve or prevent specific policy outcomes.

For example, in 1991 the conference opposed legislation that was then pending to permit victims of gender-motivated violence to go to federal court and sue their attackers for damages. The chief justice himself, in his 1991 year-end report, criticized the bill for creating a "new private right of action so sweeping, that the legislation would involve the federal courts in a whole host of domestic relations disputes." Three years later, in somewhat modified form, the bill was enacted as the Violence Against Women Act. In 2000 the chief justice wrote a majority opinion for the Court invalidating the law's new damages remedy on the ground that Congress lacked the constitutional authority to enact it (*United States v. Morrison*).

The annual report "on the Federal Judiciary" was an innovation of Chief Justice Warren E. Burger. He began giving the reports in 1970, his first full year on the bench, and often delivered them in the form of a speech to the January meeting of the American Bar Association. The timing coincided roughly with the president's State of the Union speech. Burger's successor, William Rehnquist, dropped the personal appearance, instead issuing a written report every New Year's Eve, a tradition that Chief Justice John Roberts has continued.

Although most functions of the chief justice's office are unseen by the public, the relatively recent tradition of the annual report serves to underscore the symbolic role the chief justice plays as the public embodiment of the third branch. It is the chief justice who hosts visiting judges of other constitutional courts. It is the chief justice who stands at the center of the quadrennial inaugural ceremony, administering the oath of office to the president. In January 2005, Chief Justice Rehnquist, who was critically ill with thyroid cancer and had not appeared in public for three months, left his sickbed

The chief justice

briefly to perform this function at President George W. Bush's inauguration for his second term. It was Rehnquist's last public appearance outside the Court; he died six months later, at the age of eighty, in his thirty-third year as a justice.

Although it is customary to refer to a given period in Supreme Court history by the name of the then-incumbent chief justice, not all seventeen chief justices have left an equal mark on public consciousness. The Vinson Court (Chief Justice Fred M. Vinson, 1946–53) did not make much of an impression, while the Warren Court that immediately succeeded it (1953–69) decidedly did. Even though Justice William J. Brennan Jr. was the engineer of a number of Warren Court landmarks, Chief Justice Warren's name is firmly attached to the era during which a liberal majority of the Supreme Court harnessed the Constitution as an instrument of social change.

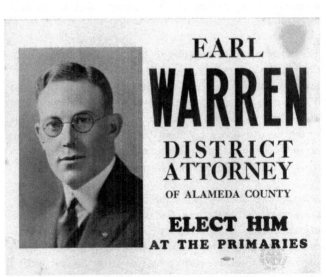

6. Earl Warren was an active politician, never a judge, before becoming Chief Justice in 1953. This poster is from early in his successful career in elective office in California. He later served three terms as the state's governor.

"Besides the functions themselves, the incumbent's influence depends on the use he makes of them and the manner in which they are discharged," one scholar of the Court observed a generation ago. "Beyond all this is the human factor, the intangibles, the personality—the moral energy the man at the center releases."

The legacy of a former president, William Howard Taft, is the most indelible of any chief justice in modern times, because it consists not simply of cases but of marble (the Supreme Court Building itself) and of the Court's authority to manage its own workload. In the Judiciary Act of 1925, which Taft championed as chief justice, Congress gave the Court wide discretion over its docket. (The law is often referred to as the Judges' Bill, reflecting the fact that the justices themselves had a large hand in drafting it.) No longer were the justices obliged to decide all properly presented appeals. The impact on the institution was transformative. In an article several months after the change took effect, Chief Justice Taft described the philosophy behind allowing the justices to choose which cases to decide. "The function of the Supreme Court is conceived to be, not the remedying of a particular litigant's wrong," Taft wrote, "but the consideration of cases whose decision involves principles, the application of which are of wide public or governmental interest, and which should be authoritatively declared by the final court." He then listed examples of the types of cases with which the Court should concern itself: "issues of the federal constitutional validity of statutes, federal and state, genuine issues of constitutional right of individuals, the interpretation of federal statutes when it will affect large classes of people, questions of federal jurisdiction, and sometimes doubtful questions of general law of such wide application that the Supreme Court may help to remove the doubt."

In other words, the Court would no longer serve as the passive recipient of whatever legal dispute a disappointed litigant chose to bring through the door. It would no longer be simply the judicial system's top appeals court. The justices would decide which cases—which issues—were important enough to warrant their attention, and thus the attention of the country. The new Judiciary Act contained this notice to those who would approach the Supreme Court seeking a "writ of certiorari," the technical term for an order accepting a case for decision: "A review on writ of certiorari is not a matter of right, but of sound judicial discretion, and will be granted only where there are special and important reasons therefore." The Supreme Court would now be master of its own fate, but more than that. It was now in a position to set the country's legal agenda.

Chapter 5
The Court at work (2)

In addition to giving the Court authority to control its own docket, Chief Justice Taft also left a legacy in marble: the building into which the justices moved in 1935, five years after Taft's death and 145 years after the Supreme Court had first convened. Acquiring a home of its own would have both symbolic and practical importance for the Court, signifying its role at the head of a coequal branch of government, and finally providing chambers for the justices, who until then had worked from home.

Until his death, Chief Justice Taft was actively involved in the project as chairman of the congressionally authorized Supreme Court Building Commission. He proposed the site, across the street from the Capitol's east front and next to the Library of Congress. He chose the architect, Cass Gilbert Sr., a noted architect who had designed many important public buildings, including both the United States Custom House and the federal courthouse in New York City. Gilbert's sixty-six-story Woolworth Building, also in New York, remained the tallest building in the world for nearly twenty years after its completion in 1913.

The chief justice told Gilbert to design "a building of dignity and importance," and the architect followed his instructions. The building is a Greek temple in classic Corinthian style, with sixteen marble columns at the main west entrance. The pediment contains a sculpture group representing "Liberty Enthroned, guarded by Order and Authority." Until 2010, visitors to the Court climbed the stairs from the front plaza and entered the building under the words "Equal Justice Under Law," carved on the architrave. Over the objection of some of his colleagues, who regarded the measure as unnecessary and its symbolism unfortunate, Chief Justice Roberts ordered the front entrance closed for security reasons. Visitors now enter through a screening area under the stairs.

The courtroom itself, at the end of a main-floor corridor known as the Great Hall, is an imposing yet unexpectedly intimate space, measuring eighty-two by ninety-one feet. The lectern where a lawyer stands when arguing a case is surprisingly close to the

7. The laying of the cornerstone of the Supreme Court Building, October 13, 1932. Chief Justice Charles Evans Hughes presided. Chief Justice Taft, who was responsible for the building, and Cass Gilbert Sr., who designed it, had both died.

justices on their raised bench. Lawyers who have attained a certain comfort level at the Court sometimes say that when an argument is flowing well, it can almost seem as if they and the justices are engaged in conversation. In addition to seats reserved for members of the Supreme Court bar, the courtroom has seats for three hundred members of the public, who can attend arguments on a first-come, first-served basis. The Court maintains two public lines, one for tourists who simply want to observe the Court in action for a few minutes, and one for those who want to attend an entire hour-long argument. For important cases, members of the public start lining up outside the building well before dawn.

The Court's public argument sessions represent only the tip of the iceberg of the process of deciding cases. The justices sit to hear cases only for approximately forty days a year. They sit in two-week blocs (Monday, Tuesday, and Wednesday, usually only in the morning) in each month from October through April. Unless the

8. Taken from above, this unusual view of the Supreme Court chamber shows the slightly curved bench. The seats in front of the bronze railings are reserved for members of the Supreme Court bar.

Court directs otherwise, an argument lasts for one hour, thirty minutes to a side. On this schedule, the justices can hear about eighty cases during a term, although the number in recent years has been in the low seventies.

Experienced lawyers know to expect many interruptions. It is not unusual for the justices to ask dozens of questions during an argument. (In 2019, the justices decided that oral arguments would benefit from some uninterrupted time during which lawyers could actually state their case; they announced that they would refrain from asking questions during the first two minutes of each side's argument.) The Court's rule regarding argument informs lawyers: "Oral argument should emphasize and clarify the written arguments in the briefs on the merits. Counsel should assume that all Justices have read the briefs before oral argument. Oral argument read from a prepared text is not favored." Successful Supreme Court advocates are not only fast on their feet; they have thought deeply about the place their case occupies in the broader legal universe, and they understand that what the justices want from the argument is assurance about the larger consequences of ruling for one side or the other. What are the likely implications for the next case, and the case after that? The justices see themselves as engaged in an exercise much more consequential than resolving a dispute between two warring parties. To test the implications of a lawyer's argument, justices will often vary the actual facts in order to pose intricate hypothetical questions—to which "Your Honor, that is not my case" is not an acceptable answer.

Many of the lawyers who argue before the Court are familiar to the justices as repeat players, appearing several times each term, year in and year out. Prominent among this group are the members of the Office of the Solicitor General, a unit in the Justice Department that represents the federal government in the Supreme Court. The solicitor general, required by statute to be "learned in the law," is nominated by the president and confirmed by the Senate. Aside from the solicitor general's principal deputy, the other two dozen lawyers in the office are civil servants who often remain on the job through several presidential administrations. Many are former Supreme Court law clerks who, when they do leave the office, may go on to join established Supreme Court practices or to develop one of their own. One alumnus of the solicitor general's office who followed this path with notable success is Chief Justice Roberts. Justice Kagan

MONDAY, DECEMBER 11, 2000

CASE FOR ARGUMENT TODAY

MR. THEODORE B. OLSON Washington, D. C. (35 minutes - for petitioners)	No. 00-949.　　　　(1) **GEORGE W. BUSH AND RICHARD CHENEY,** 　　　　　　Petitioners	
MR. JOSEPH P. KLOCK, JR. Miami, Fla. (10 minutes – for respondents Katherine Harris, et al., in support of petitioners)	V.	1 and ½ hours for argument.
MR. DAVID BOIES Armonk, N. Y. (45 minutes – for respondents)	ALBERT GORE, JR., ET AL.	

9. This is a "day call," the calendar for the day's arguments. Here, the argument was *Bush v. Gore,* the case that was to determine the outcome of the 2000 presidential election. The two presidential contenders were each represented by experienced Supreme Court advocates, Theodore B. Olson for Governor Bush and David Boies for Vice President Gore. Joseph P. Klock Jr., arguing on behalf of Florida's secretary of state, Katherine Harris, was making his first Supreme Court argument. The justices allotted an extra thirty minutes beyond the usual one hour.

actually served as solicitor general herself before President Obama nominated her to the Court.

While argument sessions present the Court's public face, the Court's substantial work takes place for the most part behind the scenes. It begins with the case-selection process. In recent terms, the Court has received about sixty-five hundred petitions for review. These are called petitions for a writ of certiorari, a Latin word meaning to be informed of or made certain of. More casually and commonly, requests for Supreme Court review are referred to as cert petitions. The Court's rules require a petition to follow a particular format. First come the "questions presented for review," which "should be short and should not be argumentative or repetitive." The Court's Rule 14 sternly instructs lawyers that the "failure of a petitioner to present with accuracy, brevity, and clarity whatever is essential to ready and adequate understanding of the points requiring consideration is sufficient reason for the Court to deny a petition."

The entire presentation must be succinct, at no more than nine thousand words, not counting an appendix that contains the lower courts' opinions. Unless the Court grants an extension, the petition must be filed within ninety days of the judgment that is being appealed.

The Court's disposition of these requests is a matter of complete discretion. (A small subset of cases reaches the Court not as cert petitions but as "jurisdictional statements." As a technical matter, these require the justices to take some action: either dismiss the appeal; decide the case summarily, without opinion; or "note jurisdiction" and hear the case, proceeding as they would with any other case. The jurisdictional fine points are beyond the scope of this book. Suffice it to say that this once important category of "mandatory appeals" is now limited almost entirely to cases arising under the Voting Rights Act. In the mid-1980s, Congress yielded to the justices' request to eliminate most of the other mandatory categories, leaving the Court with even more discretion.)

Rule 10 of the Court's rules informs petitioners that "review on a writ of certiorari is not a matter of right, but of judicial discretion" and that a petition "will be granted only for compelling reasons." The rule then provides examples of "the character of the reasons the Court considers." The examples center around the existence of a conflict among the lower federal courts or the state courts on "an important federal question." A provision of the Internal Revenue Code or any other federal statute ought to mean the same thing in the First Circuit, which sits in Boston, as in the Seventh Circuit, which sits in Chicago. By the same token, a clause of the United States Constitution ought not to be interpreted differently by the Supreme Court of California and by New York's highest court, its Court of Appeals. (State courts, of course, are free to interpret their own state's constitutions to give more protection—but not less—to individual rights than the U.S. Constitution provides.) Lawyers striving to persuade the Supreme Court to take a case try hard to demonstrate that a conflict of the sort discussed in Rule 10 actually exists. Even so, whether the question of law is sufficiently "important" to warrant the Court's attention is completely up to the justices.

By a customary "rule of four," it takes the votes of four justices to accept a case for argument and decision—to "grant cert." Since four is, of course, one short of a majority, this necessarily evokes strategic behavior in close cases about which justices feel particularly strongly. Suppose four justices are persuaded that a petition should be granted because they believe the lower court's decision was seriously mistaken. If they are uncertain about the eventual availability of a fifth vote, they might pass up the opportunity to grant the case, rather than have it decided in a way that creates the "wrong" rule for the entire country. Political scientists call this a "defensive denial." More often, however, justices may view the eventual outcome as less important than the need to resolve a conflict among the lower courts and establish a uniform rule for the whole country, particularly in cases of statutory interpretation. If Congress disagrees with the Supreme Court's decision in a statutory case, it remains free to overturn the decision by amending the statute.

Sifting through thousands of petitions a year in order to select the dozens that will be granted is a daunting task for a nine-member court. In the mid-1970s, with the number of petitions growing rapidly, the justices found a way to lighten the load by organizing their energetic young law clerks into a "cert pool." Under this arrangement, each petition is reviewed by a single law clerk on behalf all the justices who subscribe to the pool. This clerk writes a memo that summarizes the lower court decision and the arguments for and against review, concluding with a recommendation. The recommendation is only that. Most justices in the pool (all but one or two in recent years) assign one of their own four law clerks to review the pool recommendations from the individual justice's own perspective. Even so, the cert pool has come in for criticism. Critics maintain that the system not only increases the likelihood of missing important cases, but that it tends to exacerbate a built-in bias toward denying cases. Under this theory, law clerks are afraid to embarrass themselves with a recommendation to grant, either because the justices might reject the recommendation or, even worse, might accept the case only to find that a procedural flaw requires a belated dismissal. Defenders of the system maintain that these concerns are exaggerated. They say that any issue of real importance is bound to reach the Court multiple times, and will be noticed eventually.

A more subtle critique—actually, more of an observation—of the quality of the Court's agenda-setting process comes from scholars who point out that the cases the Court adds to its docket tend either not to reflect the issues that the public perceives as the most important, or to represent such an atypical slice of a big issue as to offer little help in resolving more typical cases. In 2007, for example, the Court decided its first case in a decade about the free-speech rights of public school students, an issue of substantial concern in communities across the country. But the Court chose an idiosyncratic case, *Morse v. Frederick,* concerning the punishment of a student who displayed an ambiguously worded banner that might or might not have expressed a favorable view on illegal drug use. The eventual decision provided little guidance to school districts dealing with much more common disputes over student speech about politics, school policy, or sexual orientation. As one leading Supreme Court scholar, Sanford Levinson, has noted, Supreme Court cases necessarily deal only with the "litigated Constitution," those provisions that are open to interpretation and become fodder for lawyers and judges. At the same time, the "hard-wired Constitution," structural elements of great significance like the over-representation of small states in the United States Senate, remain beyond the reach of any court. "The fixation on the litigated Constitution," Levinson writes, leads people to "overestimate the importance of courts and judges, for good and for ill."

Another critique heard with increasing frequency is that justices select cases with a particular goal in mind—in other words, that they use their agenda-setting power to advance a particular agenda. A dramatic example came in 2018 when the Court, by a vote of 5 to 4, ruled that the First Amendment's rights of free speech and association meant that public employees could not be required to pay the share of union dues that unions spend on collective bargaining and on carrying out their legal duty to represent the interests of all employees in the bargaining unit, even those who choose not to join the union. In this decision, *Janus v. American Federation of State, County, and Municipal Employees*, the Court overturned a 1977 precedent (*Abood v. Detroit Board of Education*) that had rejected a First Amendment challenge to the "agency fee" system under which employees who object to union membership can refrain from joining but can still be required to pay a share of the dues that go to the services from which all benefit. The *Janus* decision was the culmination of a multiyear, multicase effort, led by Justice Alito, to find the right vehicle to attract a majority of the Court to the new anti-union position. Cases the Court had accepted first in 2012 and then again in 2014 and 2016 fell short of accomplishing that goal. In her dissenting opinion, Justice Kagan was unusually direct in her assessment of what had occurred. "Today, the Court succeeds in its six-year campaign to reverse *Abood*," she declared bluntly.

When the Court denies review of a case, it neither sets a precedent nor indicates agreement with the lower court's judgment, points that are often misunderstood. There are many reasons that a petition might end up as "cert denied." These include not only the occasional defensive denial but, more often, the absence of a real conflict or even a real legal issue (many petitions attempt to reargue the facts of a case) or the justices' conclusion that a case with an interesting issue is nonetheless a "poor vehicle" due to any of a number of procedural problems. Occasionally, one or more justices will attach a "statement respecting the denial of certiorari" to the bare order by which the Court announces the denial; in explaining why the case was inappropriate for a grant, a statement of this sort can serve as an invitation to bring the Court another case on the same issue.

All cert petitions are presumed to be denied unless the justices take further action. The first step is to move a petition from what is known informally as the "dead list" and to place it on the "discuss list" for consideration at the justices' weekly conference. The chief justice is in charge of the discuss list and runs the conference, at which the justices speak and eventually vote in order of seniority. (The same procedure applies to the discussion and vote on cases that were argued during the week.) The conference usually takes place on Friday (Thursday in May and June), with the "orders"—the list of cases granted and denied— being issued the following Monday. The Court typically provides no explanation for either a grant or a denial. But occasionally, the order list will include an opinion by one or more justices dissenting from a denial of certiorari and explaining why the case should have been accepted. These opinions can offer a window on the case-selection process that usually bears no semblance of transparency.

By statute, a Supreme Court term begins on the first Monday of every October. But the justices' active labor actually begins the week before, on the last Monday of September, when they meet in conference to consider the cert petitions that have accumulated over the summer months of recess. There is no statutory date for the term to end. The justices aim for the last week in June and nearly always achieve that goal. Barring an emergency, no arguments are held after the end of April, so the justices spend May and June working on opinions in any cases from the term's seven argument sittings that remain undecided. (To keep this system running, new cases that are granted after January are not scheduled for argument until the following fall, after the next term begins.) Unlike many other courts that fall behind by carrying cases over from one term to the next, the Supreme Court remains rigorously current. Any cases the justices don't decide by the end of the term must be set for a complete new argument in the following term. This discipline-imposing rule has the effect of influencing the justices to work particularly hard in June to finish all the term's work. This in turn gives rise to the unflattering phrase, "June opinion," to describe a hastily crafted opinion that still has a few seams showing. That epithet is heard less frequently these days than it was a few decades ago, when the Court typically decided 140 or 150 cases a year rather than the current 65 or 70.

June often sees such a high proportion of a term's most important decisions that many people assume that the justices somehow arrange to save the best for last. This is far from the truth. The Court usually begins to issue opinions in November and proceeds to hand down opinions throughout the term. But naturally, the least controversial cases, those that produce unanimous or near-unanimous decisions, get decided first. Complicated cases or those that, for one reason or another, produce numerous concurring and dissenting opinions take longer, perhaps much longer, and only the pressure of an impending July 4 weekend may spur the justices to make the last-minute compromises necessary to bring a decision out by the end of June.

Opinions are announced in open court immediately before the start of the day's arguments. The justice who has written the majority opinion delivers a brief summary. A dissenting justice who feels particularly strongly might follow with a summary of the dissent. The statements that justices make from the bench are not part of the official opinion, but the few points that a justice might choose to emphasize from a long opinion can be illuminating for those present. The courtroom announcements are the first official word that a case has been decided; unlike many other courts, the Supreme Court gives no advance notice that a case will be decided on a particular day. Once announced, the opinions appear within minutes on the Court's website (*www .supremecourt.gov*). The Court also posts transcripts of the arguments on a daily basis. Each Friday, the website makes available the audio of the arguments the justices heard during the week.

In recent years, the Internet has brought the Court much closer to the public than seemed possible even a few years earlier. Among other resources available on the website are the cert petitions, which the Court posts as they are filed, and the briefs filed in granted cases. The Court's electronic docket thus offers a complete procedural history of each case, whether granted or denied. With a few mouse clicks, people can now acquire information about the Court's docket and operations that once required a trip to the clerk's office.

The ground floor of the Supreme Court Building includes a press room. The Court makes copies of petitions and briefs available to the press, and seats are set aside for reporters at all arguments. Television journalists are part of the Supreme Court press corps, but the Court does not permit television or other cameras in the courtroom. Justice David H. Souter once declared that television cameras would roll into the courtroom over his dead body. While few justices might express their objections that graphically, there were none on that occasion, or since, who leapt to television's defense.

Chapter 6

The Court and the other branches

To the extent that it conveys the image of the three branches of the federal government, each operating in its own sphere, the phrase "separation of powers" is misleading. A more accurate image is one of dynamic interaction, in which the Supreme Court is an active participant. Even when relations among the president, Congress, and the Court appear peaceful, there is often tension beneath the surface, reflecting not dysfunction so much as distinct institutional limits, perceptions, and responses to events. When relations deteriorate, as they have periodically, what starts as disequilibrium can take the form of a power struggle. Not only the Court but the judiciary as a whole is a player in interbranch relations, with significant tools at its disposal. Its challenge, its "abiding dilemma," in the words of Stephen B. Burbank, a leading scholar of the judiciary, is "participating in a political system without becoming the victim of politics."

As Burbank points out, relations between the branches are governed as much by norms and customs as by formal structures. The Constitution permits Congress to impeach and remove federal judges, for example, but the norm is that impeachment is reserved for criminal behavior or serious ethical lapses, and not for judicial rulings with which members of Congress disagree.

10. On January 14, 2009, six days before their inauguration,
President-elect Obama and Vice President-elect Biden visit the justices
in their private conference room. From *left* to *right*: the president-
elect; Chief Justice John G. Roberts Jr., Justice John Paul Stevens;
Justice Ruth Bader Ginsburg; Biden; Justice David H. Souter; Justice
Anthony M. Kennedy; Justice Antonin Scalia; Justice
Stephen G. Breyer. Absent are Justices Clarence Thomas and
Samuel A. Alito Jr.

Cases that have placed the justices at odds with Congress or the
White House provide a prism through which to examine the
Court's relationship to the other branches. There is inherent
drama to a major Supreme Court case in which the powerful
institutional actors include the Court itself. Some will emerge as
winners and some as losers. But it is important to recognize that
outside the courtroom, in less dramatic ways, the Court
continually interacts with the other branches. The Court submits
its annual budget request to Congress, and the justices take turns
going before the relevant congressional subcommittees to testify
about the Court's fiscal needs. Congress determines the salaries of
the justices and all federal judges. When John Roberts became
chief justice, he made it a priority to persuade the president and

Congress of the need for a long-deferred pay raise for federal judges, an effort that succeeded after several years.

The attorney general, along with the chairmen and ranking members of the Senate and House Judiciary Committees, travel to the Court twice yearly to meet with the chief justice and members of the Judicial Conference. The agenda for these private sessions includes pending legislation and broader questions of policy. The Court in turn is invited every January to hear the president deliver the State of the Union message to a joint session of Congress. The appearance of at least some justices, if not the entire Court, at this event was once routine. But in January 2010, President Obama used the occasion to criticize the Court for a decision issued a week earlier that gave corporations an expanded right under the First Amendment to spend money on political campaigns. As the television cameras swung to the justices, Justice Alito was seen mouthing the words "not true" in response to the president's characterization of the decision, *Citizens United v. Federal Election Commission* (2010). Chief Justice Roberts later wondered aloud whether justices should continue to attend, saying that he had found the scene "very troubling," more like a "pep rally" than a state occasion. As the date for the 2011 State of the Union message approached, there was widespread speculation: Would the justices come or would they stay away? Justice Alito chose to spend the day in Hawaii. But Chief Justice Roberts and five other members of the Court did attend, and the president greeted them as he walked past their seats to the podium. In recent years, fewer than half the justices have attended.

While the State of the Union episode might be described as interbranch tension as melodrama, more serious concerns are presented by repeated efforts in Congress to strip the federal courts in general or the Supreme Court in particular of jurisdiction to decide specific kinds of cases. Southerners and other conservatives in Congress responded to the decisions of the Warren Court by introducing bills to strip the Court of jurisdiction over school desegregation, state legislative apportionment, and anti-Communist loyalty and security matters. Other targets of congressional anger and proposed jurisdiction-stripping have included cases concerning prayer and recitation of the Pledge of Allegiance in public schools, as well as public display of the Ten Commandments. In recent years, criminal sentencing has been a source of tension between Congress and the federal judiciary. Senior Republican members of Congress have accused federal judges of undue leniency in sentencing. In 2003 Congress enacted a law requiring federal courts to provide Congress with reports on sentences that fell below the range set by federal sentencing guidelines. Chief Justice Rehnquist denounced the measure, known as the Feeney Amendment, as "an unwarranted and ill-considered effort to intimidate individual judges in the performance of their judicial duties."

The Court's exercise of judicial review is an ever-present and renewable source of interbranch tension. While the court-stripping efforts were responses to the Supreme Court's constitutional rulings, Congress pushes back regularly and more productively against the Court's statutory decisions. In the early 1990s, Congress responded sharply to the Court's rightward turn in a series of civil rights cases decided several years earlier. Legislation enacted in 1990 and 1991 overturned more than a dozen Supreme Court decisions that had narrowed the reach of federal civil rights statutes.

The first bill that President Obama signed into law after taking office in January 2009 was the Lilly Ledbetter Fair Pay Act, enacted to overturn a 2007 Supreme Court ruling in an employment discrimination case. The Lilly Ledbetter episode is a useful example of the way in which a Supreme Court decision can propel an issue onto the country's political agenda as well as its legal one. Lilly Ledbetter was a supervisor in a tire factory, the only woman to hold that position. She learned only after she retired that for years she had been paid less than any of the men.

She brought suit under Title VII of the Civil Rights Act of 1964, which bars discrimination in the workplace on the basis of race and sex. The statute requires a lawsuit to be filed within 180 days of a "discriminatory act." Although the employer's discrimination against Ledbetter had begun years earlier, her lawyers argued that she was entitled to pursue her lawsuit under an interpretation of the 180-day time limit asserted by the federal agency in charge of administering the statute. Under the agency's "paycheck accrual" rule, the clock started to run again each time the employer issued a paycheck that reflected the discriminatory treatment. Most of the federal circuits had endorsed the agency's interpretation, but the Atlanta-based Eleventh Circuit, which heard Ledbetter's case, rejected the agency's rule, overturning a $3 million jury verdict in her favor and dismissing the lawsuit.

In a 5 to 4 decision, *Ledbetter v. Goodyear Tire & Rubber Co.* (2007), the Supreme Court agreed. The majority relied on earlier Supreme Court decisions that had applied Title VII's 180-day limit to other discriminatory actions in the workplace, including termination, failure to promote, and failure to hire. The same rule should apply in the "slightly different context" of unequal pay, Justice Alito wrote for the majority. For the dissenters, Justice Ginsburg objected that the context was in fact crucially different. She said that while termination and failure to hire or promote are public acts, easily ascertained, employees of most private companies have no way of knowing what their fellow workers are being paid. Because Ledbetter received periodic raises along with the other employees, Justice Ginsburg observed, she had no reason to suspect that by the end of her career, her pay was as much as 40 percent less than that of her male co-workers.

Justice Ginsburg took the unusual step of announcing her dissent from the bench. Her action raised the decision's visibility, converting what might otherwise have been seen as a technical ruling about a rather obscure provision of employment law into a new front in an ideologically infused battle over civil rights and the future of the Supreme Court. Justice Alito, at the time the newest justice, appointed by President George W. Bush, had been on the bench for less than eighteen months. The justice he succeeded, Sandra Day O'Connor, would most likely have voted the other way, and the outcome would have been different. Democrats in Congress began an immediate effort to overturn the decision by amending Title VII. Republicans in the Senate blocked the amendment's passage in the spring of 2008. Lilly Ledbetter, an accidental heroine if there ever was one, became a powerful symbol of all that progressives feared from the newly consolidated Roberts Court and from the prospect of a Republican victory in the 2008 election. In the summer of 2008, Ledbetter addressed the Democratic National Convention, winning pledges of a renewed effort in Congress. The momentum carried the bill through Congress and onto the new president's desk.

During the term that followed the uproar over its Ledbetter decision, with the issue of employment discrimination suddenly prominent, the Supreme Court appeared newly solicitous of workers with job discrimination complaints. A majority ruled in employees' favor in several cases.

The Ledbetter episode came and went quickly. It is entirely predictable that other discrete disputes over the intent of Congress and the meaning of federal statutes will similarly come and go in the future. But there exists a more profound constitutionally based struggle between the Court and Congress over the boundaries of congressional lawmaking authority, with origins deep in the country's history. While it flares up and then recedes periodically, this struggle has no apparent end. Perhaps it is hardwired into the constitutional design.

Two periods sixty years apart provide bookends to an account of deep conflict between the political branches and the Supreme Court in the modern era. The first was the struggle over the New Deal. During President Franklin D. Roosevelt's first term, a conservative majority on the Supreme Court invalidated major portions of the new administration's economic recovery program. The Court held that a dozen acts of Congress, including the National Industrial Recovery Act and the Agricultural Adjustment Act, were beyond congressional authority either to regulate interstate commerce or to provide for the general welfare. The time had come, Roosevelt declared, "where we must take action to save the Constitution from the Court."

In early 1937, following his reelection, Roosevelt proposed the Judiciary Reorganization Bill, more familiarly known as his "court-packing plan." Under this proposal, the president could appoint a new justice for every justice over the age of seventy who had not retired—six new justices, given the age of the incumbents. The proposal sparked enormous controversy and failed when the Senate Judiciary Committee rejected it. Yet because the Court quickly began to uphold key New Deal provisions, including the Social Security Act and the highly pro-labor National Labor Relations Act, Roosevelt is regarded as having prevailed. Not for almost sixty years, a period that witnessed a dramatic expansion of the federal government's presence in American life, would the Supreme Court again invalidate an act of Congress on the ground that the legislation exceeded the congressional commerce power.

When the battle resumed in 1995, the Court's target was an obscure federal statute that barred possession of guns near school buildings. Since every state had a similar law, the fate of the federal law, the Gun-Free School Zones Act, was of little moment. Nonetheless, the decision invalidating the statute, *United States v. Lopez,* ushered in the Rehnquist Court's federalism revolution. Writing for the majority, Chief Justice Rehnquist said that to uphold the statute would be to blur the "distinction between what is truly national and what is truly local." This analysis implied an end to the long period during which the Court permitted Congress to decide for itself whether the distinction between national and local mattered for any particular piece of legislation. The vote was

5 to 4, with the dissenters quick to point out the implications. Justice Souter warned that "it seems fair to ask whether the step taken by the Court today does anything but portend a return to the untenable jurisprudence from which the Court extricated itself almost sixty years ago."

There followed, in quick succession, a series of closely divided decisions that constricted congressional authority not only under the Commerce Clause but also under the Fourteenth Amendment. Section 5 of the Fourteenth Amendment gives Congress "the power to enforce, by appropriate legislation, the provisions of this article"—namely, the guarantees of due process and equal protection provided by the amendment's Section 1. The question that came to the fore as the federalism revolution of the 1990s proceeded was the meaning of "enforce" and the breadth of Congress's Section 5 authority. Was Congress's power limited to enforcing only those interpretations of due process and equal protection that had been adopted by the Supreme Court? Or did Congress have substantive authority to legislate on the basis of its own constitutional views?

This issue was joined in a dispute over protection for the free exercise of religion that first divided the justices and then became the source of conflict between the Court and Congress. In a 1990 decision, the Court had withheld protection from individuals who claimed that their religious beliefs required an exemption from a generally applicable law. In that case, *Employment Division, Department of Human Resources of Oregon v. Smith,* the Court ruled that two members of the Native American Church who had used the hallucinogenic drug peyote in religious rituals were not constitutionally entitled to unemployment benefits when they were fired for violating their employer's rule against drug use.

Religious groups across the spectrum, from liberal to conservative, were highly critical of this decision, which they viewed as weakening the Free Exercise Clause of the First Amendment.

Congress responded promptly by passing a statute, provocatively titled the Religious Freedom Restoration Act (RFRA). The new law provided that a statute that appeared neutral on its face could not be applied in a way that placed a burden on the practice of religion unless the government could show that the burden served a "compelling interest." A Roman Catholic parish in Boerne, Texas invoked RFRA, seeking to demolish an old church that was protected under a historic preservation code in order to build a new and bigger one. The church argued that RFRA entitled it to an exemption from the code. In response, the city argued the Religious Freedom Restoration Act was unconstitutional. The Section 5 enforcement power entitled Congress to enact legislation to remedy a violation of a constitutional right, the city argued, but not to legislate a more expansive definition of the right itself than the Supreme Court had provided.

In a 6 to 3 decision, *City of Boerne v. Flores* (1997), the Supreme Court agreed with the city. Congress's enforcement power was merely "remedial and preventive," the Court said, rejecting "any suggestion that Congress has a substantive, nonremedial power under the Fourteenth Amendment." The majority opinion, written by Justice Kennedy, struck a formal separationist tone. "When the Court has interpreted the Constitution, it has acted within the province of the Judicial Branch, which embraces the duty to say what the law is," Justice Kennedy wrote, invoking the familiar words of Chief Justice Marshall in *Marbury v. Madison*. He concluded: "Broad as the power of Congress is under the Enforcement Clause of the Fourteenth Amendment, RFRA contradicts vital principles necessary to maintain separation of powers and the federal balance." The decision left RFRA in force for the federal government. In the aftermath, some two dozen states enacted their own versions of RFRA to enable their residents to raise free exercise claims in state court under state law.

The Rehnquist Court majority used similar interpretations of Section 5 and of the Commerce Clause to overturn other statutes, including the Violence Against Women Act, which permitted women who were victims of gender-motivated violence to sue their attackers in federal court (*United States v. Morrison*, 2000). The Court also ruled that states could not be bound, as employers, by the federal laws against employment discrimination, either on the basis of age (*Kimel v. Florida Board of Regents*, 2000) or on the basis of disability (*Board of Regents of the University of Alabama v. Garrett*, 2003).

Then in 2003, led by Chief Justice Rehnquist himself, the Court unexpectedly reversed course, turning back a similar constitutional challenge to the Family and Medical Leave Act. The law required state employers, along with private employers, to give their employees time off to attend to family emergencies. States that failed to follow the law were not immune from suit, Chief Justice Rehnquist wrote for the majority. With this decision, *Nevada Department of Human Resources v. Hibbs*, the federalism revolution appeared to have run its course. But history teaches that any apparent hiatus in the contest between the Court and Congress is only temporary.

The contest resumed in 2012 with a challenge to the constitutionality of the Affordable Care Act ("Obamacare"). The Court's decision that the requirement for individuals to buy health insurance was constitutional resolved only part of the case, *National Federation of Independent Business v. Sebelius*. The Court also had to decide whether Congress had the authority to require states to expand broadly the category of individuals eligible for subsidized medical care under the Medicaid program. Medicaid is a shared federal–state program that both levels of government jointly pay for; the federal government sets the rules with which state Medicaid programs must comply in order to qualify for the federal contribution. The Affordable Care Act provided that the federal government would reimburse states for the cost of the eligibility expansion, while also requiring states to accept the expansion or forfeit the federal share of their entire Medicaid program. The Court deemed this bargain to have crossed the line between inducement and coercion and declared that Congress lacked authority to require the Medicaid expansion on those terms. As a result, Medicaid expansion was rendered voluntary and the issue became highly political. While most states accepted the expansion, along with the accompanying federal money, more than a dozen states with Republican governors and legislatures rejected the bargain and left millions of their citizens outside the Medicaid program.

Recent struggles between the Court and the president have deep roots as well as current resonance. President Andrew Jackson's often-quoted response to a Supreme Court decision favoring the Cherokee Indians—"John Marshall has made his decision. Now let him enforce it"—is in fact probably apocryphal. But it has lingered in the public imagination because it so well captures what we suppose presidents have wished they could say to the Supreme Court. Richard Nixon, ordered to surrender the incriminating Watergate tapes (*United States v. Nixon*, 1974), and Bill Clinton, deprived of immunity from a civil lawsuit by a woman claiming sexual harassment (*Clinton v. Jones*, 1997) are among the chief executives who come to mind. President Trump expressed fury at the Supreme Court's invalidation of his administration's plan to add a citizenship question to the 2020 Census (*Department of Commerce v. New York*, 2019).

The Supreme Court's response to President Truman's intervention in a wartime labor dispute in 1952 remains, more than half a century later, the symbol of the Court's power to reject an urgent claim of presidential authority. Much more than a symbol, in fact: the Steel Seizure case, as *Youngstown Sheet & Tube Co. v. Sawyer* is commonly known, was cited by the Court a half century later in resisting presidential claims of unilateral authority over detention policy at Guantanamo Bay.

Under Truman's order, the federal government took control of the nation's steel mills to forestall a steelworkers' strike that could have shut down the country's armament-making capacity in the midst of the Korean War. The industry went to Federal District Court to challenge the action. The case moved forward with a great sense of urgency, proceeding from the filing of the lawsuit to the final Supreme Court decision in less than two months. The Court, all the members of which had been appointed by Roosevelt and Truman, ruled against the president by a vote of 6 to 3. Justice Hugo L. Black's majority opinion rejected the president's claim that despite the absence of explicit statutory authority, his power to act was inherent in Article II of the Constitution. Justice Robert H. Jackson joined that opinion while also filing a separate concurring opinion. It is the Jackson opinion that is most often cited as defining the boundaries of presidential authority.

Justice Jackson divided the universe of possible presidential actions into three categories, which he described as "a somewhat over-simplified grouping of practical situations in which a president may doubt, or others may challenge, his powers." First, "When the president acts pursuant to an express or implied authorization of Congress, his authority is at its maximum, for it includes all that he possesses in his own right plus all that Congress can delegate." Second, Justice Jackson defined a "zone of twilight" in which "the president acts in absence of either a congressional grant or denial of authority." He then "can only rely upon his own independent powers," and whether that reliance is legitimate "is likely to depend on the imperatives of events and contemporary imponderables rather than on abstract theories of law." Finally, "When the president takes measures incompatible with the expressed or implied will of Congress, his power is at its lowest ebb." Jackson placed the steel seizure in the third category, finding that Congress had enacted three statutes that were inconsistent with the president's action. "The executive action we have here originates in the individual will of the president and represents an exercise of authority without law," he concluded.

Like President Truman, the second President Bush claimed that Article II itself gave him the authority to establish military commissions for the war-crimes trials of individuals held as enemy combatants at the United States naval station at Guantanamo Bay. And like the Court in the Steel Seizure case, the five justices in the majority in *Hamdan v. Rumsfeld* (2006) concluded that the claim of inherent authority was insufficient. In his majority opinion, Justice Stevens mentioned the Steel Seizure decision in a footnote. Justice Kennedy, in a concurring opinion joined by three other members of the majority, relied explicitly on Jackson's Steel Seizure framework. Rather than place the president's military commissions in Jackson's second category (congressional silence), Justice Kennedy found that the commissions as designed by the president came within Jackson's third category: presidential actions that were incompatible with explicit provisions of federal law.

The *Hamdan* case was neither the Court's first encounter with the Bush administration's detention policies, nor its last. Two years earlier, in *Rasul v. Bush* (2004), the Court rejected the administration's effort to place the detainees beyond the jurisdiction of federal judges. The Court ruled that the military base in Cuba was functionally part of the United States, and thus that as a matter of statutory interpretation, federal courts had jurisdiction under the habeas corpus statute to hear the cases in which hundreds of detainees were challenging the basis for their open-ended confinement. Eventually, with Congress and a frustrated president working together, Congress stripped the federal courts of jurisdiction to hear any habeas corpus petition filed by a Guantanamo detainee. In *Boumediene v. Bush*, decided in 2008 by a vote of 5 to 4, the justices declared this court-stripping provision to be unconstitutional.

This intense cycle of action and reaction, the ball passing rapidly back and forth between the Court and the political branches, then came to a pause. The Court accepted no further cases from

Guantanamo, content to let the lower courts handle the habeas corpus petitions that the *Boumediene* decision had enabled. As a new president took up residence in the White House, cases reflecting domestic rather than foreign policy concerns began to fill the judicial pipeline and the struggle resumed. In 2014, the Court invoked the Religious Freedom Restoration Act to restrict the Obama administration's effort to ensure that women covered by employee health plans under the Affordable Care Act could receive free birth control coverage. The Court ruled in favor of the owner of a nationwide chain of hobby stores who claimed that his religious objection to birth control meant that he should not have to include the benefit in his plan (*Burwell v. Hobby Lobby Stores, Inc.*).

The Trump administration's decision to limit entry into the United States by residents of predominantly Muslim countries returned the Court's focus to foreign affairs. This time, the president prevailed. The Immigration and Nationality Act delegated broad authority to the president, the Court held in *Trump v. Hawaii* (2018), ruling that the travel ban fell within "the deference traditionally accorded to the president in this sphere." No one could suppose that this 5-to-4 decision, or any other, would represent the last word in the age-old contest between the Supreme Court and the president.

Chapter 7
The Court and the public

Judges "do not stand aloof on these chill and distant heights,"
Benjamin N. Cardozo once said. "The great tides and currents
which engulf the rest of men do not turn aside in their course and
pass the judges by." Cardozo was a state court judge, not yet a
Supreme Court justice, when he delivered those words in 1921, at
the conclusion of a series of lectures on "the nature of the judicial
process." His words ring true these many years later, while also
hinting at a mystery. Given that judges, Supreme Court justices
among them, live in the world, how do their perceptions shape
their judging? More specifically, what is the relationship between
the Supreme Court and the public?

Justices themselves have had something to say on this subject.
"We all rely on public confidence and trust to give the courts'
decisions their force," Justice O'Connor said in a lecture on "public
trust as a dimension of equal justice." She explained: "We don't
have standing armies to enforce opinions, we rely on the
confidence of the public in the correctness of those decisions.
That's why we have to be aware of public opinions and of attitudes
toward our system of justice, and it is why we must try to keep and
build that trust."

Chief Justice Rehnquist said it would be "remarkable indeed" if
judges were not influenced by the broad currents of public

opinion. "Judges, so long as they are relatively normal human beings, can no more escape being influenced by public opinion in the long run than can people working at other jobs," he said in a lecture on "constitutional law and public opinion." Further, he added, "if a judge on coming to the bench were to decide to seal himself off hermetically from all manifestations of public opinion, he would accomplish very little; he would not be influenced by current public opinion, but instead would be influenced by the state of public opinion at the time he came to the bench."

In their somewhat different formulations, these judicial colleagues with distinct approaches to judging were in agreement that a judge's awareness of public opinion is not only inevitable but desirable, even necessary. And these two justices put their observations into practice. Chief Justice Rehnquist was for years a vigorous critic of the Court's decision in *Miranda v. Arizona*, the 1966 ruling that requires the police, before interrogating a suspect in custody, to deliver the now-familiar warnings about the right to remain silent and the right to counsel. But when the Supreme Court had the opportunity to overturn *Miranda* in 2000, the chief justice led the Court in the opposite direction. Instead of overturning *Miranda*, his majority opinion in *Dickerson v. United States* declared unconstitutional an effort by Congress to overturn the decision legislatively. "*Miranda* has become embedded in routine police practice to the point where the warning has become part of our national culture," Rehnquist wrote.

Justice O'Connor had been a critic of affirmative action throughout more than twenty years on the Court when a case arrived challenging an effort by the University of Michigan Law School to increase the racial diversity of its student body by means of an admissions policy that took into account an applicant's race. O'Connor voted to uphold the plan and wrote the Court's majority opinion in the case, *Grutter v. Bollinger* (2003). She cited briefs filed on the law school's behalf by educational leaders, corporate executives, and military officers. "In order to cultivate a set of leaders with legitimacy in the eyes of the citizenry, it is necessary that the path to leadership be visibly open to talented and qualified individuals of every race and ethnicity," is how O'Connor summarized the core of the argument for the law school's position. She left little doubt that she had been persuaded not only by this argument but by the fact that it was put forward by those representing a broad segment of elite opinion.

It is not necessary to conclude that either of these justices experienced sudden epiphanies when confronted with cases that put their own frequently expressed principles to a concrete and highly visible test. The point is rather that each considered the case at hand not as an abstract legal proposition but as a dispute arising in a social and political as well as legal context. It is not necessary to agree with either outcome—indeed, Rehnquist dissented in the Michigan case and denounced the law school's admission plan as "a naked effort to achieve racial balancing"—in order to appreciate that the majority in both saw itself as navigating on a sea of public opinion.

Scholars regard the relationship between the Supreme Court and public opinion as elusive. Lee Epstein and Andrew D. Martin, two leaders in the empirical study of judicial behavior, titled an article: "Does Public Opinion Influence the Supreme Court? Possibly Yes (But We're Not Sure Why)." The article surveyed the political science literature on the question, much of it inconclusive and contradictory. At best, the authors conclude, there seems to be an association between the Court and public opinion, but not enough evidence to "make the leap from association to causality," that is, to prove that public opinion actually influences the Court.

But in any event, public opinion does not travel a one-way street. While the public may influence the Court, at least some of the time, the Court may also influence the public. One classic image, dating to early in the country's history, is of the justices as teachers, "the Supreme Court as republican schoolmaster," in the phrase of a well-known article that documents the role of the early justices as they rode circuit, summarizing the law in their charges to grand juries, and serving in this manner as "teachers to the citizenry." The author concludes that "whether the justice should teach the public is not and cannot be in question since teaching is inseparable from judging in a democratic regime."

As in the Lilly Ledbetter episode (*Ledbetter v. Goodyear Tire & Rubber Co., Inc.,* 2007), a Supreme Court decision can serve as a catalyst for public debate. Sometimes a grant of cert serves that function, well before a case has been decided or even argued. The Court's willingness in the mid-1990s to consider whether the Constitution protects a right to physician-assisted suicide brought that issue from the shadows and placed it under a public spotlight. Public conversation and debate continued even after the Court answered the constitutional question in the negative in *Washington v. Glucksberg* (1997), and polls have subsequently shown steadily rising support for the ability of terminally ill people to have a doctor's assistance in ending their lives. One study of public opinion on this issue concluded: "Court cases, in this realm as in others, place a human face on an otherwise quite abstract philosophical and legal controversy."

Defenders of the Supreme Court's exercise of judicial review must occasionally contend with the criticism that it is essentially undemocratic—"counter-majoritarian"—for unelected life-tenured judges to have the last word on the constitutionality of legislation enacted by the people's elected representatives. The force of this critique waxes and wanes to the extent that the Court appears out of alignment with public opinion. It is not hard to understand why misalignment would occur with some regularity. Shifts in electoral majorities in response to changes in the public mood can occur much faster than changes on the Supreme Court, where tenures last decades. The first of Franklin D. Roosevelt's nine Supreme Court appointees, Hugo L. Black, not only outlasted the Roosevelt administration but remained on the Court through the Truman,

Eisenhower, Kennedy, and Johnson presidencies before retiring more than halfway through Richard Nixon's first term. Between mid-1994 and mid-2005, a period of considerable political turmoil, punctuated by the contested election of 2000, there were no Supreme Court vacancies at all. The justices whose behavior provoked the Roosevelt court-packing plan were criticized from the Left; the Warren Court from the Right; and the Roberts Court, to a somewhat more modulated degree, from the Left again.

And yet, over time, the Court and the public seem to maintain a certain equilibrium. Public opinion polls regularly reflect that "diffuse" approval for the Supreme Court—that is, approval of the institution in general, rather than of particular actions—is higher than for other institutions of government. Of course, that fact alone is not particularly revealing. Surveys also demonstrate repeatedly that the current state of civics education is poor, and that the general public knows very little about the Court. For example, only 55 percent of the respondents in a 2005 survey agreed that the Supreme Court can declare an act of Congress unconstitutional. (Only one-third could name the three branches of government.) So perhaps the public expression of trust in the Supreme Court reflects a leap of faith rather than actual knowledge; people want to believe in some governmental institution, and they are more likely to be able to identify what they don't like about the political branches. Or perhaps the expression of public support for the Court reflects what political scientists call the "legitimation hypothesis," the theory that once the Supreme Court rules on an issue, a measurable proportion of the public will come to the conclusion that "if they believe it, it must be right."

Or perhaps, reflecting the awareness of public opinion displayed by the justices quoted at the beginning of this chapter, the Court brings itself into alignment over time, avoiding decisions that will take it far out of the mainstream of public opinion. That would not be surprising. The political scientist Robert A. Dahl observed more than a half century ago that the Supreme Court "is an essential part of the political leadership," part of the "dominant political alliance." It was therefore understandable, Dahl said, "that the policy views dominant on the Court are never for long out of line with the policy views dominant among the lawmaking majorities of the United States."

In recent years, public opinion on the Court has become increasingly volatile and politically partisan. A mid-2019 poll by the Pew Research Center showed that 75 percent of Republicans had a favorable view of the Court, compared with only 49 percent of Democrats. By contrast, in 2015, after the Court had ruled favorably on same-sex marriage and on the Affordable Care Act, only 33 percent of Republicans reported a favorable opinion. As recently as 2016, 72 percent of Democrats had a positive view of the Court. Clearly, people are responding based on the issues that matter most to them as well as to the politics surrounding Supreme Court appointments. After Senate Republicans blocked President Obama's effort to fill a Supreme Court vacancy in 2016, leading Democrats complained that the seat that went to Neil Gorsuch had been "stolen" from the president and from his nominee, Merrick Garland. So Democrats were primed to see the Court as politicized and to see that development in negative terms.

Since the relationship between the Supreme Court and the political branches is dynamic rather than static, the Court's actions produce reactions that may in turn reflect back on the Court and, over time, move the Court in a different direction. So a presidential candidate may make the Court a target, as Richard Nixon did when he criticized the criminal procedure rulings of the Warren Court and pledged to appoint justices who would be "tough on crime." Nixon's four appointees, some of whom undoubtedly disappointed him in other respects, did over time stop the expansion of criminal defendants' rights, even if the major Warren Court rulings remained on the books.

Perhaps another way of making Robert Dahl's point would be to note that Supreme Court justices are members of the nation's elite, and they tend to share the elite's perceptions. That was almost certainly the case for the seven justices who in 1973 comprised the majority that declared a constitutional right to abortion, in *Roe v. Wade*. Four of the seven were appointees of Republican presidents and three of those—Chief Justice Warren E. Burger and Justices Lewis F. Powell Jr. and Harry A. Blackmun, the author of the majority opinion—were named to the Court by Richard Nixon. The *Roe v. Wade* majority responded to the fact that during the decade before the case reached the Court, leaders of the public health and legal professions had been calling for the decriminalization of abortion, which at the beginning of the 1960s was illegal in every state. In addition, a Gallup poll that was published in newspapers across the country while the Court was working on the case showed that a substantial majority of the public agreed with the statement, "The decision to have an abortion should be made solely by a woman and her physician." A majority of men, women, Protestants, Catholics, Democrats, and Republicans (68 percent of Republicans, compared with 59 percent of Democrats) agreed with the statement. So the justices could plausibly assume that the decision they were about to hand down would meet with general public approval—as in fact it initially did, before the abortion issue became entangled, later in the 1970s, with partisan politics and the rise of the religious Right.

The political reaction against *Roe v. Wade* built slowly. The first justice to join the Court after the January 1973 decision was John Paul Stevens, named by President Gerald Ford in December 1975. Yet remarkably enough, the nominee was not asked a single question about abortion during his confirmation hearing. If the senators' questions during a Supreme Court confirmation hearing provide a reliable window onto the country's law-related concerns, then it is reasonable to conclude that abortion had not yet become a national political issue nearly three years after the Court's decision.

During the 1980s, however, the Court came under increasing pressure to repudiate *Roe v. Wade*. First the Reagan administration and then the administration of President George H. W. Bush asked the Court to overturn the decision, on five separate occasions. In 1980 the Republican Party's platform had called for the first time for the appointment of judges "who respect traditional family values and the sanctity of innocent human life." With new Supreme Court appointments during the ensuing decade, the margin of support within the Court for maintaining the right to abortion appeared to shrink to the vanishing point.

This was the context in which the Court, on the eve of the 1992 presidential election, confronted a challenge to a restrictive Pennsylvania abortion law. The case, it was clear to all, was a potential vehicle for overturning *Roe v. Wade*. The votes appeared to be there. Yet the Court, to the surprise of nearly everyone, declined to take that step, instead reaffirming the "essential holding" of the 1973 decision by a vote of 5 to 4 in *Planned Parenthood of Southeastern Pennsylvania v. Casey* (1992). In an unusual joint opinion by Justices O'Connor, Kennedy, and Souter—all post-1980 Republican appointees—the majority described the pressure on the Court and explained why "principles of institutional integrity" required that *Roe v. Wade* be reaffirmed. A "terrible price would be paid for overruling," the three justices wrote, adding that such a step "would seriously weaken the Court's capacity to exercise the judicial power and to function as the Supreme Court of a Nation dedicated to the rule of law."

The joint opinion is so revealing of the Court's view of its connection to the public that it is worth quoting at some length:

The root of American governmental power is revealed most clearly in the instance of the power conferred by the Constitution upon the Judiciary of the United States and specifically upon this Court. As Americans of each succeeding generation are rightly told, the Court cannot buy support for its decisions by spending money and, except to a minor degree, it cannot independently coerce obedience to its decrees. The Court's power lies, rather, in its legitimacy, a product of substance and perception that shows itself in the people's acceptance of the Judiciary as fit to determine what the Nation's law means and to declare what it demands.

The opinion went on to say that "to overrule under fire in the absence of the most compelling reason to reexamine a watershed decision would subvert the Court's legitimacy beyond any serious question." Then, it continued:

The promise of constancy, once given, binds its maker for as long as the power to stand by the decision survives and the understanding of the issue has not changed so fundamentally as to render the commitment obsolete....

A decision to overrule *Roe*'s essential holding under the existing circumstances would address error, if error there was, at the cost of both profound and unnecessary damage to the Court's legitimacy, and to the Nation's commitment to the rule of law. It is therefore imperative to adhere to the essence of *Roe*'s original decision, and we do so today.

The *Casey* decision sparked strong dissent within the Court as well as sustained criticism from outside. It did not, as the three justices explicitly hoped, relieve pressure on the Court or cause those who sought *Roe*'s repudiation to withdraw. Abortion cases continue to reach the Court as abortion opponents search for the right vehicle to accomplish their goal. And significantly, none of the three Republican-appointed justices who wrote the *Casey* joint opinion remains on the Court; Justice O'Connor's and Justice Kennedy's successors, Samuel Alito and Brett Kavanaugh, are well to their right on this and other issues. The *Casey* decision is not the Court's last work on abortion. Nonetheless, acutely self-conscious and somewhat overwrought in tone as it is, the decision stands as a fascinating example of the Court's response to a perceived threat to its own legitimacy in the eyes of the public.

To return to Robert Dahl's observation about the Court as a reflection of the elite consensus in American society, some scholars have recently pointed out that rather than a force for stability, elites now function as engines of polarization. A book by Neal Devins, a law professor, and Lawrence Baum, a political scientist (*The Company They Keep: How Partisan Divisions Came to the Supreme Court*, 2019), argues that their divergent social networks are driving liberals and conservatives ever further apart and arming them with contrasting views of the country and the forces shaping it.

There was nothing subtle about the *Casey* decision. The issue was familiar, and the Court knew where the support and the attacks were coming from. But suppose an issue is relatively novel, or reaches the Court in a new or unfamiliar context. Where can justices turn for knowledge that they themselves lack?

The obvious answer lies with the parties themselves and the briefs they submit in advance of the argument. But just as cert petitions have word limits (9,000 words), so do the briefs on the merits that the parties submit once a case is granted (13,000 words for each side, plus an extra 6,000 words for the petitioner to file a reply brief). Often, the parties consume nearly all the allotted space in setting out the background of the case and the legal arguments. There is little room left for what the justices may most want to know: the larger context, the implications of ruling for one side or the other.

This is where the *amicus curiae,* the friend of the court, comes in. Assuming each side agrees to the other's list of *amici*, as is almost always the case, there is no upper limit on the number of "friends" the parties can marshal. (The Court itself can grant or withhold permission for an *amicus* filing if there is a dispute between the parties over the issue.) While an *amicus* is, of course, primarily a friend of the particular party in support of which it is submitting a brief, the phrase "friend of the court" is not a misnomer. An informative *amicus* brief does the justices a favor by presenting, within a 9,000-word limit, useful and relevant information that supplements, without duplicating, the information in the party's brief. Justice O'Connor's reliance on the *amicus* briefs in the University of Michigan Law School admissions case is an example of how important these filings can be. The helpful potential of a good *amicus* brief is not lost on the lawyers who appear before the Court, and the number of such briefs has grown substantially. While there were only fifteen *amicus* briefs filed in *Roe v. Wade*, today there are often at least that many in fairly routine cases, and in major cases the number runs into the dozens. *Amicus* briefs are often used by interest groups to stake out a public position in cases within the group's area of interest. The brief can then be distributed to members and potential donors as a way of indicating that the group is a player on the Supreme Court stage.

The solicitor general's office, which represents the federal government as a party in many of the Court's cases, is also an active *amicus*, informing the justices of the potential impact on federal programs in cases that do not involve the government directly. In order to evaluate the advisability of filing a brief, the solicitor general's office has a system for learning which federal agencies might have a stake in the outcome of a pending non-federal case. But no system is perfect, and a recent failure illustrates what can happen when the justices unknowingly rely on partial information.

In *Kennedy v. Louisiana*, a case decided in 2008, the question was whether it was constitutional to impose the death penalty for the rape of a child if the crime did not also involve murder. Years earlier, shortly after restoring capital punishment, the Court had ruled in *Coker v. Georgia* (1977) that the death penalty was not constitutionally acceptable for the rape of an adult woman. Louisiana was one of a handful of states that sought to extend its death penalty, beyond murder, to child rape. Was such a penalty one of the "cruel and unusual punishments" that the Eighth Amendment prohibits?

As in other categorical challenges to the application of the death penalty, the Court surveyed the sentencing landscape. With only six states imposing capital punishment for the rape of a child, the majority concluded that there was a national consensus against this use of the death penalty. The vote to declare the Louisiana law unconstitutional was 5 to 4. Writing for the majority, Justice Kennedy noted that while Congress had expanded the federal death penalty during the 1990s, none of the new applications involved the rape of a child. The observation bolstered the majority's conclusion.

But the observation was incorrect. Neither the parties, nor the solicitor general, nor any of the *amici* were aware that only two years earlier, Congress had made the rape of a child subject to the death penalty for members of the armed forces governed by the Uniform Code of Military Justice. This inconvenient fact came to light after the Court had delivered its decision and recessed for the summer. Both Louisiana and the solicitor general's office filed briefs asking the justices to reconsider the case. Briefs flew back and forth for weeks. Eventually, the Court announced that it would stand by its decision.

In addition to institutional embarrassment in many quarters, there was a particular irony to this failure of information. The Court's Eighth Amendment jurisprudence depends to a considerable measure on the justices' assessment of public opinion as reflected in statutes. A punishment that is demonstrably "unusual" is deemed constitutionally problematic. On this basis, the Court has invalidated the death penalty for mentally retarded defendants who commit murder (*Atkins v. Virginia*, 2002) as well as for youthful killers (*Roper v. Simmons*, 2005). But this type of analysis depends on accurate information. The Court is vitally interested in public opinion, but it can't read minds. Like the rest of us, the justices only know what they learn on their own or what someone tells them.

Chapter 8
The Court and the world

During the first decades after independence, some legislators and other leaders of the new United States were eager to insulate the country's legal system against corruption from the old regimes of Europe. Between 1799 and 1810 the legislatures of New Jersey, Kentucky, and Pennsylvania passed statutes forbidding the state courts from citing any cases decided by English courts after July 4, 1776. In private correspondence, Thomas Jefferson supported the effort to rid American courts of English law.

But even then, the American attitude toward foreign law was ambivalent, hardly universally hostile. The first paragraph of the Declaration of Independence, after all, referred to "a decent respect for the opinions of mankind." The Federalist Papers contain references to more than five hundred foreign place-names. Early Supreme Court opinions included abundant references to foreign law, and accounts of Napoleon's legal reforms in France were widely circulated. Much later, twentieth-century Americans watched with pride as the nations of Europe followed the U.S. model in embracing the idea of a constitutional court, empowered to invalidate legislation deemed incompatible with the country's basic charter. As these courts spread their wings in new post–World War II or post–Cold War democracies, it was common for their judges to invoke U.S. Supreme Court precedents. But despite widespread respect for the Supreme

Court, no country has simply imported the American experience wholesale. While the Framers of the U.S. Constitution had little in the way of practical experience to guide them, the architects of the new constitutional systems could evaluate the strengths and weaknesses of the American experience. The choices they made are illuminating.

For example, no country in the world has chosen to bestow life tenure on its judges. A single nonrenewable term is the most common model. The fifteen members of the Italian Constitutional Court serve for nine years, whereas the sixteen justices of the Federal Constitutional Court in Germany serve for twelve. South Africa's Constitutional Court, which was created by the post-apartheid constitution in 1994 and quickly established itself in the forefront of constitutional courts, has twelve-year terms for its eleven justices.

While a complete inventory of the judicial tenure of the world's constitutional courts is beyond the scope of this book, these examples demonstrate that other countries have seen little to emulate in the U.S. model of life tenure. Not coincidentally, the confirmation battles that mark the U.S. judicial selection process, even for lower court judges, are largely absent. This is undoubtedly due in large measure to differences in the rules for selecting and confirming judges. In Germany, for example, confirmation requires a two-thirds majority, a rule that effectively mandates political compromise at the beginning of the process. But the scheduled turnover created by term limits also contributes to the lowered temperature by removing the prospect that a political party temporarily in power can exercise long-lasting control over the judiciary.

Another difference is that European courts, at least, tend to observe a norm of unanimity. Separate opinions are disfavored and, in some countries, even officially forbidden. When judges are permitted to note a dissenting view, they are often required to do so anonymously. Oral arguments are rare. Taken as a whole, rules like these make it less likely that judges will take on the role of public—or polarizing—personalities.

Comparisons that focus on structure are inherently incomplete, because both substantive law and the domestic political context in which it evolves obviously differ across borders. These variations, along with the fact that the jurisprudence of some foreign courts has moved in a more liberal direction even as U.S. courts have become more conservative, accounts for the recent controversy in the United States over the propriety of federal judges citing non-U.S. judicial rulings in their own opinions. Citing foreign law, both Justice Scalia and Chief Justice Roberts have complained, is like looking out over a crowd and picking out one's friends—selecting those opinions most compatible with a desired result.

Critics have focused on three Supreme Court opinions decided between 2002 and 2005. All three moved the law in a progressive direction, with the majority opinions citing the views of foreign courts or lawmakers. These foreign sources were clearly not invoked as determinative of the meaning of the U.S. Constitution, nor could they have been. But mere mention of the foreign materials provoked anger by framing the question of how to interpret the Constitution in a global context of evolving views on human dignity. Two of the decisions concerned capital punishment. The Court held in *Atkins v. Virginia*, in 2002, that the Eighth Amendment's prohibition of cruel and unusual punishment barred the execution of intellectually disabled offenders. The majority mentioned a brief on the defendant's behalf by the European Union. Three years later, in *Roper v. Simmons*, the Court barred the execution of those convicted of having committed a capital crime before the age of eighteen. In this case, the majority cited European *amicus* briefs as well as the United Nations Convention on the Rights of the Child, a treaty that the United States has not ratified.

In between those two decisions, the Court ruled in *Lawrence v. Texas* (2003) that a Texas law criminalizing homosexual sodomy was unconstitutional. That decision overturned a seventeen-year-old precedent (*Bowers v. Hardwick,* 1986) and marked a constitutional turning point for LGBT rights. The majority opinion cited the English law that decriminalized sodomy in 1967 as well as a similar 1981 ruling by the European Court of Human Rights.

These decisions sparked a strong negative response from conservatives in Congress. In 2004, after the *Atkins* and *Lawrence* rulings, the chairman of the House Judiciary Committee, F. James Sensenbrenner, a Republican from Wisconsin, addressed the members of the Judicial Conference, gathered for their spring meeting at the Supreme Court. "Inappropriate judicial adherence to foreign laws or legal tribunals threatens American sovereignty, unsettles the separation of powers carefully crafted by our Founders, and threatens to undermine the legitimacy of the American judicial process," the congressman told Chief Justice Rehnquist and the other judges. He warned that Congress would soon examine the issue. Other congressional Republicans raised the threat of impeachment, warning that they regarded citing foreign law as incompatible with the reference in Article III to "good behavior."

This controversy did not appear to change any minds on the Supreme Court. Justices who supported acknowledging foreign sources of law continued to do so, while those who opposed the practice continued to criticize it. Talk of impeachment faded as congressional attention shifted to other targets. No member of Congress threatened to impeach Justice Breyer for a book he published in 2015, *The Court and the World: American Law and the New Global Realities.* Justice Breyer argued that in today's world, for one country's judges to take account of how other countries' courts have dealt with similar problems is not only desirable but also inevitable. In the same year he published the

11. People wait through the night to pay respects to Justice Thurgood Marshall, lying in repose in the Court's Great Hall, January 27, 1993.

book, Justice Breyer wrote a dissenting opinion in a death penalty case, invoking international practice as part of his argument that the moment had come for the Court to reconsider its position on capital punishment (*Glossip v. Gross*, 2015). Justice Breyer noted that 137 nations have abolished the death penalty and that in 2013 the United States was one of only 22 countries to have carried out an execution.

It is uncertain whether the public as a whole even paid attention to the debate over citing international law that at least for a time captivated legal and political circles in Washington. What is clear, however, is that even though most people know little about the Supreme Court and may never hold a Supreme Court opinion in their hands, the Court occupies a place in the public imagination. The large crowd that gathered for the laying of the cornerstone in 1932 came to celebrate the Court's long-delayed arrival at a home of its own. The people who waited outside the Court through a cold winter night in 1993 to pass by Justice Thurgood Marshall's casket were also, in their way, celebrating: the life of a man who had inspired the Court as a lawyer and served it as a justice. Although other nations choose features of the Court to reject as well as to emulate, as they tailor their constitutional courts to their own needs, it is still the Supreme Court of the United States that looms over the world's inner landscape. The Framers expected as much. In a landmark opinion of the early Court (*Martin v. Hunter's Lessee*, 1816), Justice Joseph Story described the Supreme Court's power to decide cases "in the correct adjudication of which foreign nations are deeply interested." They still are.

Appendix 1
U.S. Constitution, Article III

Section 1. The judicial power of the United States, shall be vested in one Supreme Court, and in such inferior courts as the Congress may from time to time ordain and establish. The judges, both of the supreme and inferior courts, shall hold their offices during good behavior, and shall, at stated times, receive for their services, a compensation, which shall not be diminished during their continuance in office.

Section 2. The judicial power shall extend to all cases, in law and equity, arising under this Constitution, the laws of the United States, and treaties made, or which shall be made, under their authority;—to all cases affecting ambassadors, other public ministers and consuls;—to all cases of admiralty and maritime jurisdiction;—to controversies to which the United States shall be a party;—to controversies between two or more states;—between a state and citizens of another state;—between citizens of different states;—between citizens of the same state claiming lands under grants of different states, and between a state, or the citizens thereof, and foreign states, citizens or subjects.

In all cases affecting ambassadors, other public ministers and consuls, and those in which a state shall be party, the Supreme Court shall have original jurisdiction. In all the other cases before mentioned, the Supreme Court shall have appellate jurisdiction, both as to law and fact, with such exceptions, and under such regulations as the Congress shall make.

The trial of all crimes, except in cases of impeachment, shall be by jury; and such trial shall be held in the state where the said crimes shall have been committed; but when not committed within any state, the trial shall be at such place or places as the Congress may by law have directed.

Section 3. Treason against the United States, shall consist only in levying war against them, or in adhering to their enemies, giving them aid and comfort. No person shall be convicted of treason unless on the testimony of two witnesses to the same overt act, or on confession in open court.

The Congress shall have power to declare the punishment of treason, but no attainder of treason shall work corruption of blood, or forfeiture except during the life of the person attainted.

Appendix 2
The Supreme Court's rules

Excerpts from the Rules, effective July 2019

Rule 10. Considerations Governing Review on Certiorari

Review on a writ of certiorari is not a matter of right, but of judicial discretion. A petition for a writ of certiorari will be granted only for compelling reasons. The following, although neither controlling nor fully measuring the Court's discretion, indicate the character of the reasons the Court considers:

(a) a United States court of appeals has entered a decision in conflict with the decision of another United States court of appeals on the same important matter; has decided an important federal question in a way that conflicts with a decision by a state court of last resort; or has so far departed from the accepted and usual course of judicial proceedings, or sanctioned such a departure by a lower court, as to call for an exercise of this Court's supervisory power;

(b) a state court of last resort has decided an important federal question in a way that conflicts with the decision of another state court of last resort or of a United States court of appeals;

(c) a state court or a United States court of appeals has decided an important question of federal law that has not been, but should be, settled by this Court, or has decided an important federal question in a way that conflicts with relevant decisions of this Court.

A petition for a writ of certiorari is rarely granted when the asserted error consists of erroneous factual findings or the misapplication of a properly stated rule of law.

Rule 13. Review on Certiorari: Time for Petitioning

1. Unless otherwise provided by law, a petition for a writ of certiorari to review a judgment in any case, civil or criminal, entered by a state court of last resort of a United States court of appeals (including the United States Court of Appeals for the Armed Forces) is timely when it is filed with the Clerk of this Court within 90 days after entry of the judgment....

2. The Clerk will not file any petition for a writ of certiorari that is jurisdictionally out of time...

3. The time to file a petition for a writ of certiorari runs from the date of entry of the judgment or order sought to be reviewed...

5. For good cause, a Justice may extend the time to file a petition for a writ of certiorari for a period not exceeding 60 days.... An application to extend the time to file a petition for a writ of certiorari is not favored.

Rule 14. Content of a Petition for a Writ of Certiorari

1. A petition for a writ of certiorari shall contain, in the order indicated:

   (a) The questions presented for review, expressed concisely in relation to the circumstances of the case, without unnecessary detail. The question should be short and should not be argumentative or repetitive.... The questions shall be set out on the first page following the cover, and no other information may appear on that page. The statement of any question presented is deemed to comprise every subsidiary question fairly included therein. Only the questions set out in the petition, or fairly included therein, will be considered by the Court....

3. A petition for a writ of certiorari should be stated briefly and in plain terms....

4. The failure of a petitioner to present with accuracy, brevity, and clarity whatever is essential to ready and adequate understanding of the points requiring consideration is sufficient reason for the Court to deny the petition.

Rule 28. Oral Argument

1. Oral argument should emphasize and clarify the written arguments in the briefs on the merits. Counsel should assume that all Justices have read the briefs before oral argument. Oral argument read from a prepared text is not favored....

Appendix 3
Chart of the Justices

Nominating President/ Justice	Oath Taken	Term End	Years of Service
George Washington			
John Jay *	Oct. 19, 1789	R June 29, 1795	6
John Rutledge	Feb. 15, 1790	R Mar. 5, 1791	1
William Cushing	Feb. 2, 1790	D Sept. 13, 1810	21
James Wilson	Oct. 5, 1789	D Aug. 21, 1798	9
John Blair	Feb. 2, 1790	R Oct. 25, 1795	6
James Iredell	May 12, 1790	D Oct. 20, 1799	9
Thomas Johnson *	Aug. 6, 1792	R Jan. 16, 1793	1
William Paterson	Mar. 11, 1793	D Sept. 9, 1806	13
John Rutledge *†	Aug. 12, 1795	R Dec. 15, 1795	.3
Samuel Chase	Feb. 4, 1796	D June 19, 1811	15
Oliver Ellsworth	Mar. 8, 1796	R Dec. 15, 1800	4
John Adams			
Bushrod Washington	Feb. 4, 1799	D Nov. 26, 1829	31

Nominating President/ Justice	Oath Taken	Term End	Years of Service
Alfred Moore	Apr. 21, 1800	R Jan. 26, 1804	4
John Marshall *	Feb. 4, 1801	D July 6, 1835	34
Thomas Jefferson			
William Johnson	May 7, 1804	D Aug. 4, 1834	30
H. Brockholst Livingston	Jan. 20, 1807	D Mar. 18, 1823	16
Thomas Todd	May 4, 1807	D Feb. 7, 1826	19
James Madison			
Joseph Story	Feb. 3, 1812	D Sept. 10, 1845	34
Gabriel Duvall	Nov. 23, 1811	R Jan. 14, 1835	23
James Monroe			
Smith Thompson	Sept. 1, 1823	D Dec. 18, 1843	20
John Quincy Adams			
Robert Trimble	June 16, 1826	D Aug. 25, 1828	2
Andrew Jackson			
John McLean	Jan. 11, 1830	D Apr. 4, 1861	32
Henry Baldwin	Jan. 18, 1830	D Apr. 21, 1844	14
James M. Wayne	Jan. 14, 1835	D July 5, 1867	32
Roger B. Taney *	Mar. 28, 1836	D Oct. 12, 1864	28
Philip P. Barbour	May 12, 1836	D Feb. 25, 1841	5
John Catron	May 1, 1837	D May 30, 1865	28
Martin Van Buren			
John McKinley	Jan. 9, 1838	D July 19, 1852	15

Nominating President/ Justice	Oath Taken	Term End	Years of Service
Peter V. Daniel	Jan. 10, 1842	D May 31, 1860	19
John Tyler			
Samuel Nelson	Feb. 27, 1845	R Nov. 28, 1872	27
James K. Polk			
Levi Woodbury	Sept. 23, 1845	D Sept. 4, 1851	5
Robert C. Grier	Aug. 10, 1846	R Jan. 31, 1870	23
Millard Fillmore			
Benjamin R. Curtis	Oct. 10, 1851	R Sept. 30, 1857	5
Franklin Pierce			
John A. Campbell	Apr. 11, 1853	R Apr. 30, 1861	8
James Buchanan			
Nathan Clifford	Jan. 21, 1858	D July 25, 1881	23
Abraham Lincoln			
Noah H. Swayne	Jan. 27, 1862	R Jan. 24, 1881	19
Samuel F. Miller	July 21, 1862	D Oct. 13, 1890	28
David Davis	Dec. 10, 1862	R Mar. 4, 1877	14
Stephen J. Field	May 20, 1863	R Dec. 1, 1897	34
Salmon P. Chase *	Dec. 15, 1864	D May 7, 1873	8
Ulysses S. Grant			
William Strong	Mar. 14, 1870	R Dec. 14, 1880	10
Joseph P. Bradley	Mar. 23, 1870	D Jan. 22, 1892	21
Ward Hunt	Jan. 9, 1873	R Jan. 27, 1882	9

Nominating President/ Justice	Oath Taken	Term End	Years of Service
Morrison R. Waite *	Mar. 4, 1874	D Mar. 23, 1888	14
Rutherford B. Hayes			
John Marshall Harlan	Dec. 10, 1877	D Oct. 14, 1911	34
William B. Woods	Jan. 5, 1881	D May 14, 1887	6
James Garfield			
Stanley Matthews	May 17, 1881	D Mar. 22, 1889	7
Chester A. Arthur			
Horace Gray	Jan. 9, 1882	D Sept. 15, 1902	20
Samuel Blatchford	Apr. 3, 1882	D July 7, 1893	11
Grover Cleveland			
Lucius Q. C. Lamar	Jan. 18, 1888	D Jan. 23, 1893	5
Melville W. Fuller *	Oct. 8, 1888	D July 4, 1910	22
Benjamin Harrison			
David J. Brewer	Jan. 6, 1890	D Mar. 28, 1910	20
Henry B. Brown	Jan. 5, 1891	R May 28, 1906	15
George Shiras Jr.	Oct. 10, 1892	R Feb. 23, 1903	10
Howell E. Jackson	Mar. 4, 1893	D Aug. 8, 1895	2
Grover Cleveland			
Edward D. White	Mar. 12, 1894	P Dec. 18, 1910	17
Rufus W. Peckham	Jan. 6, 1896	D Oct. 24, 1909	13
William McKinley			
Joseph McKenna	Jan. 26, 1898	R Jan. 5, 1925	26

Nominating President/ Justice	Oath Taken	Term End	Years of Service
Theodore Roosevelt			
Oliver Wendell Holmes	Dec. 8, 1902	R Jan. 12, 1932	29
William R. Day	Mar. 2, 1903	R Nov. 13, 1922	19
William H. Moody	Dec. 17, 1906	R Nov. 20, 1910	3
William Howard Taft			
Horace H. Lurton	Jan. 3, 1910	D July 12, 1914	4
Charles E. Hughes	Oct. 10, 1910	R June 10, 1916	6
Edward D. White *†	Dec. 19, 1910	D May 19, 1921	10
Willis Van Devanter	Jan. 3, 1911	R June 2, 1937	26
Joseph R. Lamar	Jan. 3, 1911	D Jan. 2, 1916	5
Mahlon Pitney	Mar. 18, 1912	R Dec. 31, 1922	10
Woodrow Wilson			
James C. McReynolds	Oct. 12, 1914	R Jan. 31, 1941	26
Louis D. Brandeis	June 5, 1916	R Feb. 13, 1939	22
John H. Clarke	Oct. 9, 1916	R Sept. 18, 1922	6
Warren G. Harding			
William H. Taft*	July 11, 1921	R Feb. 3, 1930	8
George Sutherland	Oct. 2, 1922	R Jan. 17, 1938	15
Pierce Butler	Jan. 2, 1923	D Nov. 16, 1939	17
Edward T. Sanford	Feb. 19, 1923	D Mar. 8, 1930	7
Calvin Coolidge			
Harlan F. Stone	Mar. 2, 1925	P July 2, 1941	16

Nominating President/ Justice	Oath Taken	Term End	Years of Service
Herbert Hoover			
Charles E. Hughes * †	Feb. 24, 1930	R June 30, 1941	11
Owen J. Roberts	June 2, 1930	R July 31, 1945	15
Benjamin N. Cardozo	Mar. 14, 1932	D July 9, 1938	6
Franklin Delano Roosevelt			
Hugo L. Black	Aug. 19, 1937	R Sept. 17, 1971	34
Stanley F. Reed	Jan. 31, 1938	R Feb. 25, 1957	19
Felix Frankfurter	Jan. 30, 1939	R Aug. 28, 1962	23
William O. Douglas	Apr. 17, 1939	R Nov. 12, 1975	36
Frank Murphy	Feb. 5, 1940	D July 19, 1949	9
Harlan F. Stone * †	July 3, 1941	D Apr. 22, 1946	5
James F. Byrnes	July 8, 1941	R Oct. 3, 1942	1
Robert H. Jackson	July 11, 1941	D Oct. 9, 1954	13
Wiley B. Rutledge	Feb. 15, 1943	D Sept. 10, 1949	6
Harry S. Truman			
Harold H. Burton	Oct. 1, 1945	R Oct. 13, 1958	13
Fred M. Vinson *	June 24, 1946	D Sept. 8, 1953	7
Tom C. Clark	Aug. 24, 1949	R June 12, 1967	18
Sherman Minton	Oct. 12, 1949	R Oct. 15, 1956	7
Dwight D. Eisenhower			
Earl Warren *	Oct. 5, 1953	R June 23, 1969	15

Nominating President/ Justice	Oath Taken	Term End	Years of Service
John M. Harlan	Mar. 28, 1955	R Sept. 23, 1971	16
William J. Brennan Jr.	Oct. 16, 1956	R July 20, 1990	33
Charles E. Whittaker	Mar. 25, 1957	R Mar. 31, 1962	5
Potter Stewart	Oct. 14, 1958	R July 3, 1981	22
John F. Kennedy			
Byron R. White	Apr. 16, 1962	R June 28, 1993	31
Arthur J. Goldberg	Oct. 1, 1962	R July 25, 1965	3
Lyndon B. Johnson			
Abe Fortas	Oct. 4, 1965	R May 14, 1969	4
Thurgood Marshall	Oct. 2, 1967	R Oct. 1, 1991	24
Richard M. Nixon			
Warren E. Burger *	June 23, 1969	R Sept. 26, 1986	17
Harry A. Blackmun	June 9, 1970	R Aug. 3, 1994	24
Lewis F. Powell Jr.	Jan. 7, 1972	R June 26, 1987	16
William H. Rehnquist	Jan. 7, 1972	P Sept. 26, 1986	15
Gerald R. Ford			
John Paul Stevens	Dec. 19, 1975	R June 29, 2010	34
Ronald Reagan			
Sandra Day O'Connor	Sept. 25, 1981	R Jan. 31, 2006	24
William H. Rehnquist *†	Sept. 26, 1986	D Sept. 3, 2005	19
Antonin Scalia	Sept. 26, 1986	D. Feb. 13, 2016	30
Anthony M. Kennedy	Feb. 18, 1988	R. July 31, 2018	30

Nominating President/ Justice	Oath Taken	Term End	Years of Service
George H. W. Bush			
David H. Souter	Oct. 9, 1990	R June 29, 2009	20
Clarence Thomas	Oct. 23, 1991		
William J. Clinton			
Ruth Bader Ginsburg	Aug. 10, 1993	D Sept. 18, 2020	27
Stephen G. Breyer	Aug. 3, 1994		
George W. Bush			
John G. Roberts Jr.	Sept. 29, 2005		
Samuel A. Alito Jr.	Jan. 31, 2006		
Barack Obama			
Sonia Sotomayor	Aug. 8, 2009		
Elena Kagan	Aug. 7, 2010		
Donald J. Trump			
Neil M. Gorsuch	April 4, 2017		
Brett M. Kavanaugh	Oct. 6. 2018		
Amy Coney Barrett	Oct. 27, 2020		

* = chief justice; † = nomination for promotion to chief justice (years of service, where applicable, are as chief justice only; see prior listing for nomination and service as associate justice); D = died; P = promoted to chief justice (see separate listing for service as chief justice); R = retirement/resignation.

References

Chapter 1

The activities of the justices while riding circuit are discussed in detail in volumes 2 (1989) and 3 (1990) of *The Documentary History of the Supreme Court of the United States, 1789–1800* (New York: Columbia University Press). John Jay's letter to John Adams, declining the president's offer of resuming the position of chief justice, is reprinted in *The Correspondence and Public Papers of John Jay,* ed. Henry P. Johnson (New York: G. P. Putnam's Sons, 1890), 4:284–85. It is cited in Michael J. Klarman's interesting article, "How Great Were the 'Great' Marshall Court Decisions?" *Virginia Law Review* 87:1111, 1154, n. 226.

For a recent citation of John Marshall's famous line about the Court's "province and duty" to "say what the law is," see the Supreme Court's 2008 decision in *Boumediene v. Bush,* invalidating an act of Congress that stripped the federal courts of jurisdiction to hear cases brought by detainees at Guantanamo Bay. Writing for the majority, Justice Kennedy said that "[t]o hold the political branches have the power to switch the Constitution on or off at will . . . would permit a striking anomaly in our tripartite system of government, leading to a regime in which Congress and the President, not this Court, say 'what the law is'" [citing *Marbury*].

For a list of congressional enactments that the Supreme Court has overruled, see the *Constitution of the United States, Analysis and Interpretation,* published by the Government Printing Office and available on line at https://www.congress.gov/content/conan/pdf/GPO-CONAN-2017-11.pdf

Chapter 2

The Supreme Court's Rule 13 provides that petitions for certiorari must be filed within ninety days from the lower court's entry of "final judgment." The rule for judicial deference to an agency's plausible interpretation of an ambiguous statute is set out in *Chevron U.S. A., Inc. v. Natural Resources Defense Council* (1984). The doctrine is known as "Chevron deference."

For background on the Obamacare case and an analysis of the decision, see Nathaniel Persily, Gillian E. Metzger, and Trevor W. Morrison, eds., *The Health Care Case: The Supreme Court's Decision and Its Implications* (New York: Oxford University Press, 2013). For a discussion of the pregnancy discrimination case and its statutory context, see Gillian Thomas, *Because of Sex: One Law, Ten Cases, and Fifty Years That Changed American Women's Lives at Work* (New York: St. Martin's Press, 2016). Chief Judge Robert Katzmann of the federal appeals court in New York has contributed to the conversation about statutory interpretation with *Judging Statutes* (New York: Oxford University Press, 2014).

Chapter 3

For illustrations and analysis of the ways in which justices have shifted over time from their original ideological positions, see the article by Lee Epstein and her co-authors, "Ideological Drift Among Supreme Court Justices: Who, When, and How Important?" *Northwestern Law Review Colloquy* 101 (2007): 127–31. The scholar who identified the presence or absence of prior executive branch experience as predictive of a new Supreme Court justice's eventual ideological shift was Michael C. Dorf in his article "Does Federal Executive Branch Experience Explain Why Some Republican Supreme Court Justices 'Evolve' and Others Don't?" *Harvard Law & Policy Review* 1 (2007): 457–76. The six justices in Dorf's "no experience" group were Blackmun, Powell, Stevens, O'Connor, Kennedy, and Souter. In the "experienced" group were Burger, Rehnquist, Scalia, Thomas, Roberts, and Alito. While this study was concluded very early in the tenures of Roberts and Alito, the author noted that "preliminary evidence indicates that the pattern will also hold" for them. The scholar who examined a nominee's geographic origin as a factor was Lawrence Baum in his book *Judges and Their Audiences: A Perspective on Judicial Behavior* (Princeton, NJ: Princeton University Press, 2006). On this topic, see also my article "Change and Continuity on the Supreme Court," *Washington University Journal of Law and Policy* 25 (2007): 39–59, which focuses on the example of Harry Blackmun.

For a detailed account of the effort to impeach Justice Douglas, see David E. Kyvig's *The Age of Impeachment: American Constitutional Culture Since 1960* (Lawrence: University Press of Kansas, 2008).

On the debate over life tenure for Supreme Court Justices, see *Reforming the Courts: Term Limits for Supreme Court Justices*, ed. Roger C. Cramton and Paul D. Carrington (Durham, NC: Carolina Academic Press, 2006) and Sanford Levinson's *Our Undemocratic Constitution: Where the Constitution Goes Wrong (And How We the People Can Correct It)* (New York: Oxford University Press, 2006).

Chapter 4

Chief Justice Rehnquist was a fan of Gilbert and Sullivan, and his quip about his performance during the Clinton impeachment came from a reference to the House of Lords in one of his favorite Gilbert and Sullivan operettas, *Iolanthe*.

The study of the Chief Justice's multiple duties was presented at a 2005 symposium on "the Chief Justice and the Institutional Judiciary," sponsored by the *University of Pennsylvania Law Review*, which devoted its June 2006 issue to the papers presented at the symposium. See Judith Resnik and Lane Dilg, "Responding to a Democratic Deficit: Limiting the Powers and the Term of the Chief Justice of the United States," *University of Pennsylvania Law Review* 154 (2006): 1575–1664.

The quotation from Salmon Chase is from Alpheus Thomas Mason's article, "The Chief Justice of the United States: *Primus Inter Pares*," *Journal of Public Law* 17 (1968): 20–60. The later quotation about the "human factor" in a chief justice's influence is also from this article.

Justice Kennedy's letter to Justice Blackmun, and other correspondence among the justices relating to *Lee v. Weisman*, is in Box 586, Folder 6 of the Harry A. Blackmun Collection in the Manuscript Division of the Library of Congress.

The scholar who described the necessary attributes of a chief justice was Robert J. Steamer in his chapter titled *Judicial Leadership:*

English and American Experience, in John P. Schmidhauser, ed., *Comparative Judicial Systems: Challenging Frontiers in Conceptual and Empirical Analysis*. London: Butterworths (1987).

Chief Justice Taft's article on the Judiciary Act of 1925 was "The Jurisdiction of the Supreme Court Under the Act of February 13, 1925," *Yale Law Journal* 35 (1925): 1–12.

Chapter 5

H. W. Perry's *Deciding to Decide: Agenda Setting in the United States Supreme Court* (Cambridge, MA: Harvard University Press, 1991) introduced the phrase "defensive denial" into the literature.

For Supreme Court practitioners—although, at $525, not for the average reader—the indispensable guide to the Court's formal rules and informal procedures is Stephen M. Shapiro et al., eds., *Supreme Court Practice* (New York: BloombergBNA, 2019), now in an eleventh edition. The book is usually referred to as "Stern and Gressman," after its original editors.

Morse v. Frederick, the case concerning a student's banner with the puzzling proclamation "Bong Hits For Jesus," is discussed by Frederick Schauer in his article "Is It Important to Be Important? Evaluating the Supreme Court's Case-Selection Process," *Yale Law Journal Online* 119 (2009): 77–86. Sanford Levinson's observations about the "litigated Constitution" versus the "hard-wired Constitution" come from his article "What Should Citizens (As Participants in a Republican Form of Government) Know About the Constitution?" *William & Mary Law Review* 50 (2009): 1239–60.

Chapter 6

Stephen Burbank's article is "Judicial Independence, Judicial Accountability, and Interbranch Relations," *Georgetown Law Journal* 95 (2007): 909–27. Efforts to strip the courts of jurisdiction over controversial issues are described in the leading recent study of the relationship between Congress and the federal judiciary, Charles Gardner Geyh's *When Courts and Congress Collide: The Struggle for Control of America's Judicial System* (Ann Arbor: University of Michigan Press, 2006). The definitive account of congressional responses to the Supreme Court's statutory rulings in the modern era is an article by William N. Eskridge Jr.,

"Overriding Supreme Court Statutory Interpretation Decisions,"
Yale Law Journal 101 (1991): 331–455.

The Court's decision upholding the rights of the Cherokees and
provoking Andrew Jackson's displeasure was *Worcester v. Georgia*
(1832).

Ledbetter v. Goodyear Tire & Rubber Co., Inc. was overturned by the
Lilly Ledbetter Fair Pay Act of 2009, P.L. 111-2, 123 Stat. 5 (2009).

Chapter 7

The quotation is from Cardozo's *The Nature of the Judicial Process*,
originally delivered in 1921 as the Storrs Lectures at Yale and kept
in print since then by the Yale University Press. Justice O'Connor's
lecture was published as "Public Trust as a Dimension of Equal
Justice," *Court Review* 36 (1999): 10–13. Chief Justice Rehnquist's
comments on public opinion come from a lecture published as
"Constitutional Law and Public Opinion," *Suffolk University Law
Review* 20 (1986): 751–69.

The Epstein and Martin article, "Does Public Opinion Influence the
Supreme Court? Possibly Yes (But We're Not Sure Why)" was
published in the *University of Pennsylvania Journal of
Constitutional Law* 13 (2010): 263–81. The "republican school-
master" image is from Ralph Lerner, "The Supreme Court as
Republican Schoolmaster," *Supreme Court Review* 1967 (1967):
127–80. The study referred to on the issue of assisted suicide is
from the chapter "The Right to Die" by Joshua A. Green and
Matthew G. Jarvis, in *Public Opinion and Constitutional
Controversy*, ed. Nathaniel Persily, Jack Citrin, and Patrick J. Egan
(New York: Oxford University Press, 2008). The Persily book is
also the source for the "legitimation hypothesis" mentioned in the
text. The impact of President Nixon's four Supreme Court
appointments is the subject of Michael J. Graetz and Linda
Greenhouse's *The Burger Court and the Rise of the Judicial Right*
(New York: Simon & Schuster, 2016).

The results of the 2005 survey on public understanding of the courts
are reported by Kathleen Hall Jamieson and Michael Hennessy in
"Public Understanding of and Support for the Courts: Survey
Results," *Georgetown Law Journal* 95 (2007): 899–902. Robert
Dahl's assessment of the Court's role in the political system is from
his article "Decision-Making in a Democracy: The Supreme Court
as a National Policy-Maker," *Journal of Public Law* 6 (1957)

279–95. The 1972 Gallup Poll on attitudes toward abortion is
discussed in Linda Greenhouse and Reva B. Siegel, *Before Roe
v. Wade: Voices That Shaped the Abortion Debate Before the
Supreme Court's Ruling*. No longer in print, this book is available
as a free download from the Yale Law School Library at https://
documents.law.yale.edu/sites/default/files/beforeroe2nded_1.pdf.

The political aftermath of the abortion decision is discussed in Linda
Greenhouse and Reva B. Siegel, "Before (and After) *Roe v. Wade*:
New Questions About Backlash," *Yale Law Journal* 120 (2011):
2028–87.

The Pew Research Center, a nonpartisan research organization, tracks
public opinion on the Supreme Court and posts its findings at
https://www.pewresearch.org/search/supreme%20court. The
relationship between the Court and public opinion is discussed at
length by Barry Friedman in his book *The Will of the People: How
Public Opinion Has Influenced the Supreme Court and Shaped the
Meaning of the Constitution* (New York: Farrar, Straus and Giroux,
2009). An enlightening study of *amicus curiae* practice at the
Court by Allison Orr Larsen and Neal Devins is "The Amicus
Machine," *Virginia Law Review* 102 (2016): 1901–68.

Chapter 8

Thomas Jefferson's objection to English law is discussed by
David J. Seipp in his article, "Our Law, Their Law, History, and the
Citation of Foreign Law," *Boston University Law Review* 86
(2006): 1417–46. An article that offers a particularly useful
comparative analysis in the modern context is John Ferejohn and
Pasquale Pasquino's "Constitutional Adjudication: Lessons from
Europe," *Texas Law Review* 82 (2003–2004): 1671–1704.

Cases cited

Supreme Court opinions are published by the government in a series
of volumes called *United States Reports*. Opinions are identified by
volume and page number. Thus, the official citation for *Brown v.
Board of Education* is 347 U.S. 483 (1954); it appears beginning on
page 483 of vol. 347 of *United States Reports* and was decided in
1954. In the Court's early decades, there was no *United States
Reports,* and the volumes were known by the name of the Reporter
(originally an unofficial, unpaid position) who published them.

Thus, *Marbury v. Madison* is cited today as 1 Cranch (5 U.S.) 137 (1803) because the opinion appeared in a volume produced by William Cranch, the Court's second Reporter. (The first Reporter was Alexander J. Dallas, whose abbreviated name appears in the citations to the Court's earliest opinions.) The early volumes were retrospectively assigned "U.S." volume numbers later in the nineteenth century, after Congress appropriated money to publish the series. The Court's Reporter of Decisions, as the official position is now known, is still responsible for overseeing the publication of accurate texts of opinions. (Unfortunately, it takes several years for an opinion to receive an official "U.S." citation and to be published in *United States Reports*. In the interim, a decision is usually referred to by the citation issued to it by the West Publishing Company, which publishes the *Supreme Court Reporter* series using the designation S. Ct. So, for example, the first case on the list below, *Abood v. Detroit Board of Education*, would first have been cited as 97 S. Ct. 1782 and can still be retrieved using that citation.)

What follows are citations for all opinions mentioned in the text and in the References.

Abood v. Detroit Board of Education, 431 U.S. 209 (1977)

Atkins v. Virginia, 536 U.S. 304 (2002)

Board of Regents, University of Alabama v. Garrett, 531 U.S. 356 (2001)

Boumediene v. Bush, 553 U.S. 723 (2008)

Bowers v. Hardwick, 478 U.S. 186 (1986)

Brown v. Board of Education, 347 U.S. 483 (1954)

Burwell v. Hobby Lobby Stores, 134 S. Ct. 2751 (2014)

Chevron U.S.A., Inc. v. Natural Resources Defense Council, 467 U.S. 837 (1984)

Chisholm v. Georgia, 2 Dall. (2 U.S.) 419 (1793)

Citizens United v. Federal Election Commission, 558 U.S. 50 (2010)

City of Boerne v. Flores, 521 U.S. 507 (1997)

Coker v. Georgia, 433 U.S. 584 (1977)

Department of Commerce v. New York, 139 S. Ct. 1551 (2019)

Dickerson v. United States, 530 U.S. 428 (2000)

Employment Div., Dept. of Human Resources of Oregon v. Smith, 494 U.S. 872 (1990)

Fisher v. University of Texas (Fisher I), 133 S. Ct. 2411 (2013)

Glossip v. Gross, 135 S. Ct. 2726 (2015)

Grutter v. Bollinger, 539 U.S. 306 (2003)

Hamdan v. Rumsfeld, 545 U.S. 557 (2006)

Hayburn's Case, 2 Dall. (2 U.S.) 409 (1792)

Janus v. American Federation of State, County and Municipal Employees, 138 S. Ct. 2448 (2018)

Kennedy v. Louisiana, 554 U.S. 407 (2008)

Kimel v. Florida Board of Regents, 528 U.S. 62 (2000)

Lawrence v. Texas, 539 U.S. 558 (2003)

Ledbetter v. Goodyear Tire & Rubber Co., Inc., 550 U.S. 618 (2007)

Lee v. Weisman, 505 U.S. 577 (1992)

Marbury v. Madison, 1 Cranch (5 U.S.) 137 (1803)

Martin v. Hunter's Lessee, 14 U.S. 304 (1816)

Massachusetts v. Environmental Protection Agency, 549 U.S. 497 (2007)

Miranda v. Arizona, 384 U.S. 436 (1966)

Morse v. Frederick, 551 U.S. 393 (2007)

Murphy v. United Parcel Service, Inc., 527 U.S. 516 (1999)

National Federation of Independent Business v. Sebelius, 567 U.S. 519 (2012)

Nevada Dept. of Human Resources v. Hibbs, 538 U.S. 721 (2003)

Obergefell v. Hodges, 135 S. Ct. 2584 (2015)

Planned Parenthood of Southeastern Pennsylvania v. Casey, 505 U.S. 833 (1992)

Plessy v. Ferguson, 163 U.S. 537 (1896)

Rasul v. Bush, 542 U.S. 466 (2004)

Riley v. California, 134 S. Ct. 2473

Roe v. Wade, 410 U.S. 113 (1973)

Roper v. Simmons, 543 U.S. 551 (2005)

Scott v. Sandford, 19 How. (60 U.S.) 393 (1857)

Stuart v. Laird, 1 Cranch (5 U.S.) 299 (1803)

Sutton v. United Airlines, Inc., 527 U.S. 471 (1999)

Toyota Motor Mfg. v. Williams, 534 U.S. 184 (2002)

Trump v. Hawaii, 138 S. Ct. 2392 (2018)

United States v. Lopez, 514 U.S. 549 (1995)

United States v. Morrison, 529 U.S. 598 (2000)

United States v. Nixon, 418 U.S. 683 (1974)

Worcester v. Georgia, 31 U.S. 515 (1832)

Young v. United Parcel Service, 135 S. Ct. 1338 (2015)

Youngstown Sheet & Tube Co. v. Sawyer, 343 U.S. 579 (1952)

Further reading

General works

For a comprehensive, single-volume history of the Court, *The Supreme Court: An Essential History* by Peter Charles Hoffer, Williamjames Hull Hoffer, and N. E. H. Hull (Lawrence: University Press of Kansas, 2nd ed., 2018) is accessible and well organized by chief justice. *The American Supreme Court* by Robert G. McCloskey (Chicago: University of Chicago Press, 6th ed., 2016) is a classic work that incorporates both history and doctrine. Originally published in 1960, the book has been substantially revised by Sanford Levinson and includes a comprehensive sixty-two-page bibliographic essay. The twelfth edition of *The Supreme Court* (Washington, DC: CQ Press, 2016) by Lawrence Baum, a political scientist, places its emphasis on the Court "as an institution and in its work as a policymaker." A second edition of *The Oxford Companion to the Supreme Court of the United States* (New York: Oxford University Press), edited by Kermit L. Hall, an encyclopedic collection of short essays, was published in 2005.

The Judicial Branch, edited by Kermit L. Hall and Kevin T. McGuire (New York: Oxford University Press, 2005) and published as part of the Institutions of American Democracy series, includes essays by leading scholars that place the Supreme Court and its justices in the broader context of judicial behavior and American history and culture. The second edition of *The Oxford Guide to United States Supreme Court Decisions*, edited by Kermit L. Hall and James W. Ely Jr. (New York: Oxford University Press, 2009), is a compilation of short essays by dozens of scholars describing hundreds of the Court's most important decisions. In 1987 Chief Justice Rehnquist published *The Supreme Court*, an account of episodes in the Court's history, its major decisions, and its current operation. The book appeared in an updated edition in 2001 (New York: Random House). Although obviously no longer current, it remains a highly readable and engaging introduction to the institution.

The Supreme Court Compendium: Data: Decisions, and Developments by Lee Epstein, Jeffrey A. Segal, Harold J. Spaeth, and Thomas G. Walker (6th ed., Washington, DC: CQ Press, 2015) contains eight hundred pages of charts and tables answering nearly any data-based question one could think to ask about the Court's history, members, and caseload. It also contains interesting material about the relationship between the Court and public opinion. A book that focuses entirely on the Court and public opinion is Barry Friedman's *The Will of the People* (New York: Farrar, Straus and Giroux, 2009). The focus of *The Company They Keep: How Partisan Divisions Came to the Supreme Court*, by Neal Devins and Lawrence Baum (New York: Oxford University Press, 2019), is on the impact on the Court itself of the extreme polarization in American politics and society.

The *Congressional Quarterly*'s CQ Press has published several valuable reference books on the Court. The most comprehensive is *Congressional Quarterly's Guide to the U.S. Supreme Court* by David Savage (4th ed., 2011).

Two books about the Supreme Court have been major bestsellers. *The Brethren: Inside the Supreme Court* by Bob Woodward and Scott Armstrong (New York: Simon & Schuster, 1979) explores the tensions inside the Burger Court. Nearly thirty years later, the success of Jeffrey Toobin's *The Nine: Inside the Secret World of the Supreme Court* (New York: Doubleday, 2007) showed that the reading public had not lost its appetite for peering behind the velvet curtain. With a co-author, Michael J. Graetz, I wrote about the Court's turn to the right in *The Burger Court and the Rise of the Judicial Right* (New York: Simon & Schuster, 2016).

Although not for the casual reader, the eight-volume *Documentary History of the United States Supreme Court, 1789–1800* (New York: Columbia University Press), edited by Maeva Marcus and published over a nineteen-year period ending in 2004, is such an amazing work that it bears mention here. In reconstructing the Court's first decade through correspondence, notes, and case records, including accounts of the cases the justices decided while riding circuit, the series offers unparalleled insight into the first justices' efforts to build an institution. From vol. 1, pt. 1 of the series, this notation by the Court's clerk, dated February 1, 1790, suggests the challenge that lay ahead: "This being the day assigned by Law, for commencing the first Sessions of the Supreme Court of the United States, and a sufficient Number of the Justices to form a quorum not being convened, the Court is adjourned, by the Justices now present, untill [*sic*] to Morrow, at one of the Clock in the afternoon."

The justices

There are several useful compilations of Supreme Court biographies. The standard work is Leon Friedman and Fred L. Israel's four-volume *The Justices of the United States Supreme Court 1789–2013: Their Lives and Major Opinions* (New York: Chelsea House, 2013). Others include the *Biographical Encyclopedia of the Supreme Court: The Lives and Legal Philosophies of the Justices*, edited by Melvin I. Urofsky (Washington, DC: CQ Press, 2006) and the Supreme Court Historical Society's *The Supreme Court Justices: Illustrated Biographies, 1789–2012* (Washington, DC: CQ Press, 3rd ed., 2013), edited by Clare Cushman.

There are too many biographies of individual justices to list here. Chief Justices Marshall and Warren and Justices Holmes and Brandeis in particular have been the subject of multiple highly regarded biographies. *Scorpions: The Battles and Triumphs of FDR's Great Supreme Court Justices* by Noah Feldman (New York: Twelve, 2010) is a collective treatment of Justices Felix Frankfurter, Robert H. Jackson, William O. Douglas, and Hugo L. Black. Earl Warren, chief justice from 1953 to 1969, is the subject of Jim Newton's *Justice for All: Earl Warren and the Nation He Made* (New York: Riverhead Books, 2006).

Any account of biographical treatments of more recent justices must begin with the memoir that retired Justice John Paul Stevens published in 2019, months before his death at the age of ninety-nine. *The Making of a Justice: Reflections on My First 94 Years* (New York: Little, Brown, 2019) covers the justice's Chicago childhood, his service as a World War II codebreaker, his legal career, and important cases from each of the thirty-five terms that he served on the Supreme Court (1975–2010).

Justice Brennan: Liberal Champion by Seth Stern and Stephen Wermiel (New York: Houghton Mifflin Harcourt, 2010) is based on the authors' exclusive access to the private papers of their subject, who served thirty-three years before retiring in 1990. *Justice Lewis F. Powell, Jr.* by John C. Jeffries Jr. (New York: Charles Scribner's Sons, 1994) is the life of the justice who served from 1972 to 1987, written by a former law clerk. Another former Supreme Court law clerk, Dennis J. Hutchinson, also wrote a biography of his justice, *The Man Who Once Was Whizzer White: A Portrait of Justice Byron R. White* (New York: Free Press, 1998), taking the unusual approach of illustrating a long (thirty-one-year) Supreme Court career by focusing tightly on three Supreme Court terms, 1971, 1981, and 1991. My own *Becoming Justice Blackmun: Harry Blackmun's Supreme Court Journey* (New York: Henry Holt, 2005) recounts the justice's life and career by relying almost entirely on the massive collection of his papers at the Library of Congress. *The Rehnquist Legacy*, edited by Craig Bradley (New York: Cambridge University Press, 2006), is a collection of essays on the career of Chief Justice William Rehnquist, who died in office in 2005.

Joan Biskupic, a longtime Supreme Court journalist, is the author of four Supreme Court biographies based in part on extensive interviews with her subjects: *Sandra Day O'Connor: How the First Woman on the Supreme Court Became Its Most Influential Justice* (New York: HarperCollins, 2005), *American Original: The Life and Constitution of Supreme Court Justice Antonin Scalia* (New York: Farrar, Straus and Giroux, 2009), *Breaking In: The Rise of Sonia Sotomayor and the Politics of Justice* (New York: Farrar, Straus and Giroux, 2014), and *The Chief: The Life and Turbulent Times of Chief Justice John Roberts* (New York: Basic Books, 2019). A more recent treatment of Justice O'Connor's life is *First: Sandra Day O'Connor* (New York: Random House, 2019). Justice O'Connor published an engaging memoir of her childhood on a remote Arizona ranch, *Lazy B: Growing Up on a Cattle Ranch in the American Southwest* (New York: Random House, 2002), with her brother, H. Alan Day, as co-author. Unlike Justice Stevens, however, Justice O'Connor did not write about her life on the Supreme Court. Neither did two other justices who have published pre–Supreme Court memoirs: Justice Sotomayor, whose *My Beloved World* (New York: Random House, 2013) became a major bestseller, and Justice Clarence Thomas, whose *My Grandfather's Son: A Memoir* (New York: HarperCollins, 2007) is an account of his early life and the obstacles he faced. Two reporters from the *Washington Post,* Kevin Merida and Michael Fletcher, published a more comprehensive account of Justice Thomas's career, *Supreme Discomfort: The Divided Soul of Clarence Thomas* (New York: Doubleday, 2007). Corey Robin, a political scientist, explored the roots of Justice Thomas's jurisprudence in *The Enigma of Clarence Thomas* (New York: Henry Holt/Metropolitan Books, 2019). Public fascination with Justice Ruth Bader Ginsburg has led to two feature-length films about her life as well as several biographies, including *Ruth Bader Ginsburg: A Life* by Jane Sherron De Hart (New York: Alfred A. Knopf, 2018).

The collapse of consensus in the politics surrounding Supreme Court confirmations is the subject of Carl Hulse's *Confirmation Bias: Inside Washington's War Over the Supreme Court, From Scalia's Death to Justice Kavanaugh* (New York: Harper/HarperCollins, 2019). Two books examine the particularly contentious confirmation of Justice Kavanaugh in 2018: *Supreme Ambition: Brett Kavanaugh and the Conservative Takeover* by Ruth Marcus (New York: Simon & Schuster, 2019) and *The Education of Brett Kavanaugh: An Investigation* by Robin Pogrebin and Kate Kelly (New York: Penguin Random House, 2019). My own *Justice on the Brink: The Death of Ruth Bader Ginsburg, the Rise of Amy Coney Barrett, and Twelve Months that Transformed the Supreme Court* (New York: Penguin Random House, 2021) is an account of the Barrett nomination and the Supreme Court term that followed.

Notable treatments of the confirmation process include *The Next Justice: Repairing the Supreme Court Appointments Process* by Christopher L. Eisgruber (Princeton, NJ: Princeton University Press, 2007), which starts from the unremarkable but often overlooked premise that "[w]ithout a good understanding of what the justices do, Americans do not know whom to choose or how to evaluate the nominees whom presidents propose." The classic work on this subject, *Justices, Presidents, and Senators: A History of the U.S. Supreme Court Appointments from Washington to Clinton* by Henry J. Abraham (Lanham, MD: Rowman and Littlefield), which originally appeared in 1974 under the title *Justices and Presidents,* was published in a fifth edition in 2007. One of the first books to bring political science to bear on the subject is the highly regarded *Pursuit of Justices: Presidential Politics and the Selection of Supreme Court Nominees* by David Alistair Yalof (Chicago: University of Chicago Press, 1999). Lee Epstein and Jeffrey A. Segal also offer a political science–oriented treatment of the subject in *Advice and Consent: The Politics of Judicial Appointments* (New York: Oxford University Press, 2005).

Public interest in the role of Supreme Court law clerks is reflected in two books: *Courtiers of the Marble Palace: The Rise and Influence of the Supreme Court Law Clerk* by Todd C. Peppers (Stanford, CA: Stanford University Press, 2006); and *Sorcerers' Apprentices: 100 Years of Law Clerks at the U. S. Supreme Court* by Artemus Ward and David L. Weiden (New York: New York University Press, 2006).

The classic study of how the justices select cases and construct the Court's docket is *Deciding to Decide: Agenda Setting in the United States Supreme Court* by H. W. Perry Jr. (Cambridge, MA: Harvard University Press, 1991). Based on extensive interviews by the author, a political scientist, with justices and their clerks (quoted but not identified by name), the book reflects the inner working of the Court of more than two decades ago. But its observations about the Court's internal dynamic nonetheless remain valuable.

There is a large political science literature on how the justices actually decide the cases they have undertaken to review. *The Choices Justices Make* by Lee Epstein and Jack Knight (Washington, DC: CQ Press, 1998) examines strategic behavior among justices as they strive to accomplish their policy goals. Relying less on theory and more on narrative, *Decision: How the Supreme Court Decides Cases* by Bernard Schwartz (New York: Oxford University Press, 1996) uses internal memoranda and unpublished drafts of opinions to provide a series of portraits of the Court at work. A book aimed primarily at a student audience, *Understanding the U.S. Supreme Court: Cases and Controversies* by Kevin T. McGuire (New York: McGraw Hill, 2002), takes an unusual approach, using four cases and two fierce confirmation battles to illustrate how the Court works and the role it plays in American life. While the focus of *How Judges Think* by Richard A. Posner (Cambridge, MA: Harvard University Press, 2010) is not on the Supreme Court specifically, the author, a retired federal appeals court judge and longtime law professor, offers insights that apply to any court.

Constitutional interpretation

Books on constitutional theory fill the shelves of law school libraries, and the subject is largely beyond the scope of this book. But neither should we ignore the unusual fact that not long ago, two sitting justices entered the public space—and took to the airwaves—to debate their distinct visions of constitutional interpretation. Justice Scalia went first with his *A Matter of Interpretation: Federal Courts and the Law* (Princeton, NJ: Princeton University Press, 1997). Justice Breyer followed, first with *Active Liberty: Interpreting Our Democratic Constitution* (New York: Alfred A. Knopf, 2005) and then with *Making Our Democracy Work: A Judge's View* (New York: Alfred A. Knopf, 2010). A short yet comprehensive introduction to the main topics and debates in constitutional law is *Constitutional Law* by Michael C. Dorf and Trevor W. Morrison (New York: Oxford University Press, 2010) in the Oxford Introductions to U.S. Law series. Oxford's "Very Short Introductions" series includes *The U.S. Constitution: A Very Short Introduction* by David J. Bodenhamer (New York: Oxford University Press, 2019). At much greater length, a useful overview of how constitutional doctrine has developed through Supreme Court decisions is *Constitutional Law for a Changing America* by Lee Epstein and Thomas G. Walker (Washington, DC: CQ Press, 10th ed., 2018–2020). Though intended for the undergraduate classroom, its two volumes, *Rights, Liberties, and Justice* and *Institutional Powers and Constraints*, are amply sophisticated enough to satisfy other readers. The authors provide helpful context, from secondary sources and their own explanations, for the many opinions the book excerpts. A prominent Harvard law professor, Lawrence Lessig, has written an important book that examines the Supreme Court's experience over time in aligning constitutional interpretation with social and political change: *Fidelity & Constraint: How the Supreme Court Has Read the American Constitution* (New York: Oxford University Press, 2019). Justice John Paul Stevens offered his thoughts on the Constitution itself in *Six Amendments: How and Why We Should Change the Constitution* (New York: Little, Brown, 2014). Proposing amendments to abolish the death penalty, limit the Second Amendment, and restrict political gerrymandering, among other things, the book contains a two-part message: the Constitution needs improvement, and we honor it by striving to make it better.

Websites

The Court's own website, www.supremecourt.gov, is a user-friendly, continually updated source of information. Opinions and orders are posted within minutes after they are issued. Once a petition is docketed, the Court posts it, along with the lower court opinion, on an electronic docket. All subsequent filings are posted as soon as the Court receives them, an invaluable resource for anyone following the progress of a case, including cases that the justices do not accept for review. Transcripts of oral arguments are posted several hours after the argument has concluded. Every Friday of a week during which the justices are sitting, the Court posts the audio of all arguments heard during that week.

The website of the Oyez Project, www.oyez.org, jointly maintained by the Illinois Institute of Technology/Chicago-Kent College of Law; Cornell University's Legal Information Institute; and an organization called Justia is a free resource with a wide variety of current and historic materials, many in multimedia format. Another free site, Scotusblog, www.scotusblog.com ("Scotus" is a widely used acronym for "Supreme Court of the United States"), analyzes recent opinions, posts cert petitions and briefs, and provides a daily compilation of news and commentary about the Court. Scotusblog also posts occasional law review articles and sponsors online symposia about important decisions.

Index

Page numbers in *italics* indicate illustrations.